# POSTNATAL DEPRESSION

## The Essential Guide

**Need — 2 — Know**

**Catherine Burrows**

First published in Great Britain in 2010 by
**Need2Know**
Remus House
Coltsfoot Drive
Peterborough
PE2 9JX
Telephone 01733 898103
Fax 01733 313524
www.need2knowbooks.co.uk

Need2Know is an imprint of Forward Press Ltd.
www.forwardpress.co.uk
SB ISBN 978-1-86144-107-2
Cover photograph: Dreamstime

# Contents

# Introduction

This book is about you and the things you're feeling and experiencing. It's the book I wanted to read when I had postnatal depression. My illness taught me so many invaluable things that helped me get through life with a new baby under the clouds of postnatal depression. They are things that will stay with me forever and things that need to be shared.

This isn't cold medical evidence, it's not about turning your life into a battleground as you fight 'the illness' and it's not about my story. It's all about you, what's happening to you, how you can live with it and how those who love you can help. It gives you a glimpse of the future because at the end of all this you will be emotionally richer and stronger.

Maybe you are wondering if you have postnatal depression. Daily life wavers between feeling 100% certain that something isn't right or just trying to 'pull yourself together' and 'snap out of it'.

I wanted to include my story in the hope you might recognise yourself somewhere in my words. I hope you read and say, 'Aaah! Yes! I understand that' or, 'So it's not just me then'.

You have a baby, there's never enough time and even less energy to read a book, I understand this. You don't have to start at chapter 1 and read until you reach the end. Every chapter was written with you in mind, they are short, readable chunks of advice and ideas. Pick out chapters depending on how you feel and the issues that trouble you most on any particular day. The important thing is that you read the book, not how you read it!

You're not the first person in the world to suffer with postnatal depression and nor will you be the last. Make a cup of tea or coffee, settle the baby and have a read. Just see if there is something in my story that you identify with.

I can see the sun shining once again, the clouds have lifted and for that I thank my husband, children, family and friends for their love and support. I particularly owe so much to Lily, Nicola and Dr Caroline for their wise words, understanding and care.

## Disclaimer

This book is intended for general information about postnatal depression. It is not intended to replace professional medical advice or care. It can be used alongside professional advice but anyone with concerns about their health is strongly advised to consult a healthcare professional and/or their GP at the earliest opportunity.

# Chapter One

# My Illness

My daughter Alexandra was born after a long and painful labour. She was dragged into her life with forceps. I remember laying there just staring, my mind blank. There was no surge of love and no tears of joy. I'd watched so many births on TV in preparation for the big moment and this wasn't how it was meant to be. Where was the rush of love? I felt completely blank, shocked even. My veins were throbbing with all the drugs and I had no sense of being a mother. It felt as if I'd stopped being human and turned into an animal. Any scrap of dignity was destroyed. The birth was traumatic and shocking. I knew that something was going badly wrong in my mind.

## The way we were

Colin and I had a great marriage, built on friendship and teamwork. We seemed to have everything and it was perfect. Maybe this was part of my undoing – 'perfect' is not a way of life that sits easily with motherhood. In control of my career, I always came home to an ordered, beautiful nest with just myself and my husband to please. I was an imaginative and sensitive person, prone to thinking very deeply, analysing beyond the surface and deep down inside. As a child and a teenager I never suffered depression but my creative thinking sometimes led to darker moods, but that was all.

'I remember laying there just staring, my mind blank. There was no surge of love and no tears of joy. I'd watched so many births on TV in preparation for the big moment and this wasn't how it was meant to be.'

# Warning signals

Looking back, the warning signals began during my pregnancy. When we found out I was pregnant, my first emotion was fear. As my body changed, I hated the loss of control. I started to cry a lot. I felt ashamed of my feelings and learned to be a good actress. Pregnancy turned me into a fraud, I never felt serene, maternal, glowing, peaceful or content.

# Becoming obsessive

'It was 2am and I cried bitterly as I struggled with nappies, baby sick and sleepsuit poppers. Where were all the instructions for this tiny person?'

As the due date approached, I couldn't sleep and spent long and lonely nights in the nursery rearranging and organising continually. I took feathering the nest to new and obsessive heights. Working to create a world of perfection and order around myself, I needed to be ahead of the game for when the baby arrived. I was determined to crack motherhood from the outset. Little thoughts and fears encroached like a gathering storm. Within weeks my body needed to perform its most amazing task to date, it seemed impossible and I had no idea if I could do it.

# In hospital

When Alexandra was born, I was dumped like a parcel in an antenatal ward, after a whole day in the suffocating delivery room waiting for a bed. The ward was noisy, someone's television blared out round the clock. There was an important football tournament. Visitors gathered around the set to watch and it was like trying to recover in a pub. Alexandra was the only baby on the ward, so I was always on edge, worried she would disturb others.

This was the first time I felt like a useless mother, unable to comfort my baby. I can remember changing Alexandra in the nursery so we wouldn't disturb the others in the ward. It was 2am and I cried bitterly as I struggled with nappies, baby sick and sleepsuit poppers. Where were all the instructions for this tiny person?

# Getting home

By the time I got home, I felt emotionally bruised and shocked. The baby blues arrived but they lingered, battering me on a daily basis. A week after her birth, I was on my own at home with her – a full-time mother for the first time. I can't remember thinking there was something wrong, I just felt so low and numb, I thought if I had more sleep or if I felt more confident, everything would be okay again. It was like being a novice babysitter not a mother. Alexandra looked like a doll, dressed in white in her frilly Moses basket – exactly as I'd imagined. I expected her real mother to stop by and pick her up at any moment. There was an intense emotional detachment. When the visitors arrived in waves, I acted the part. Inside I was crying, screaming or totally hollow. If Colin was around I made constant excuses why I couldn't hold, change or feed her. Alexandra frightened me and I was reaching a terrible crisis point.

# Falling apart

By the time she was three weeks old, I knew something was badly wrong. I developed a temper. The tiniest things or a silly joke that hit a sensitive spot triggered my temper. The temper was growing alongside a deep paranoia. I was convinced that Colin privately doubted my parenting skills. When exhaustion drove me back to the safety of my duvet, I was sure Colin thought I was lazy. I believed he hated my new curves and thought I was a dreadful wife and mother. He was thinking none of those things – he could only watch helplessly as the woman he loved fell apart.

# Sleep – the great escape

Bed was the best place to be. Nothing could reach me, touch me or hurt me there. Bed made me invisible and the normal rules didn't apply, I could cease to exist and cease to hurt. One day, as I lay hiding under the duvet, Colin brought Alexandra to me. I remember her floral print dress and little white pinafore. She looked gorgeous. It was all wrong though. They were a special little unit – father and daughter, I was the awkward one, the nuisance. I was spoiling it and getting in the way of their happiness.

'If Colin was around I made constant excuses why I couldn't hold, change or feed her. Alexandra frightened me and I was reaching a terrible crisis point.'

The exhaustion was a new kind of tiredness I had never known before, constantly wanting to sleep, removed from everybody and everything. Sleeping became the strongest desire in my life. Every waking moment was a moment closer to my next sleep.

## The crisis point

The rows started. They were always sparked by my temper. The anger erupted with a force which was full of pain and resentment against the whole world and everyone in it. My emotions were so intense I could only express myself by pushing Colin into feeling the same pain. I did some dreadful things that must have hurt and frightened Colin. I locked myself in the bathroom; I walked out of the house one cold night and on one occasion pressed a knife to my wrist. I was too scared to draw blood but I wanted to show my soulmate that I needed some real help.

## The only way to go

The night I locked myself in the bathroom was as bad as it could possibly get. Colin broke the door of the bathroom down to reach me and cuddled me on the bathroom floor for ages while I cried. It was so hard to accept that we had reached such a terrible stage and even harder to work out how we had got there.

The emotions that night were truly frightening but the fear came from the fact that those feelings were totally alien. If they were alien, then they must be separate from me and there must be a way we could put things right.

The strange thing is, without such a shocking crisis, there would never have been a line to draw between the plummet downwards and the start of the long climb back to good health. Things only change when you look the very worst of it squarely in the eyes.

For weeks, the bathroom door stayed splintered, an unforgiving reminder that things needed to be repaired and made good again. It was easy to glue and nail wood back together. How do you mend a broken mind though?

Need2Know

# Breathing space

After the bathroom door incident, there was a sense of peace and quiet acceptance. We knew things had to be done now, it was just a case of finding out how we could set the ball rolling.

Oddly enough, it was an incredibly worrying time for Colin but far less so for me. I felt as though the burden I had carried since Alexandra's birth was much lighter. The pain was shared and even though you never want to inflict pain and worry on the one you love, when things get this bad it is a blessed relief.

Still the little niggles lingered in the back of my mind, I could almost hear a quiet voice repeating, 'Drama queen, drama queen', over and over.

It was quite clear that nothing would change unless we got help. The crisis point was reached – and passed and now it was time to do something about it.

# Summing Up

- I hope that by reading my story you will understand some of the things that are happening to you and realise that you are a perfectly normal human being.

- It wasn't the best start for me as a mother; I fell at the first hurdle because I always aimed for perfection. Add into the equation a difficult pregnancy and a traumatic birth and the touch paper was lit.

- I struggled through the confusion immediately after Alexandra's birth, just hoping that everything would be okay but the warning signs were already there. I was starting to retreat into the safe world of my bed and eventually reached a terrible crisis when I hit the bottom of a deep, dark well. When you hit the bottom, it's time to start scrambling back up to the top.

# Chapter Two

# The Roller Coaster of Recovery

## Help arrives

Days after the health visitor took over from the community midwife, she spotted something was wrong. Colin took some time off work to help out with the baby. Neither of us could understand what was happening but she saw something that we missed. Colin revealed I didn't want to be on my own with Alexandra and I was dreading his return to work with unnatural fear. After some questions she told us I was depressed.

It shocked me. My mind started playing games. I kept hearing my inner mind saying, 'If only this happened, or you had this, or that, or so and so would do this – everything would be different.' I still couldn't grasp I was unwell. The problem with early postnatal depression is that it wraps you up and then swallows you whole until it's impossible to tell where your mind, thoughts and reality begin and end. Which are real thoughts and which are distorted? You can identify a tumour. It can be cut out and separated from the healthy tissue. However, this illness is part of you. It riddles your entire mind, body and then invades your partner's life.

'The problem with early postnatal depression is that it wraps you up and then swallows you whole until it's impossible to tell where your mind, thoughts and reality begin and end. Which are real thoughts and which are distorted?'

## Making a recovery plan

We decided to approach the illness on all fronts. I wanted every type of help I could receive – GP, health visitor support, counselling and medication.

Next step after the health visitor was the GP. She listened and suggested a course of counselling with an in-house practitioner alongside medication. I vividly remember walking home clutching my prescription. It was such a painful day. Prozac. Had it really come to this?

## Doubts about the drugs

I was a spectacular failure. I was unable to cope like other mothers. I had to be doped with Prozac. Colin was very sceptical with the same concerns about medication that I had, and I soon realised that Prozac was not for me. Medication is trial and error – one size does not fit all. Eventually, I settled to a more even mood with Venlafaxine. It wasn't a cure but it helped muffle the pain and give my mind 'a holiday' from uncontrollable thoughts and emotions.

# Talking it over

One of my saviours was Rose, a health visitor who ran a local support group. She was my link with the outside world. For months, agoraphobic feelings had shrunk my world to nothing. I had never learned to drive, I was frightened of public transport and I was scared the baby would cry. My confidence was rock-bottom, I felt so fat and ugly and hated to be around other people. Rose explained that just for a while she would pick me up and take me to the support group. It's only short term, she would say, because soon you'll be able to make the journey under your own steam.

## My first visit to the group

On my first visit to the group, Rose entered the meeting room with me and I felt I'd come home. Everyone had their own story to tell, one by one. After the last person spoke, I cried. I felt incredibly humble and relieved that I'd found a place where we could share our lives, anguish and deepest fears. Relief flooded my mind.

I had discovered a sisterhood; they all spoke a language that I understood. Every story contained echoes of my life, it was a revelation. When Rose offered me the chance to share my story I couldn't speak quickly enough. I had only known these ladies for an hour but I already felt I shared complete honesty and allegiance with them.

# No respite

The illness continued to torture me. My thinking was obsessive, riddled with unbalanced thoughts about people and objects. My mind was trying to gain order in moments of madness and chaos and trying desperately to blame something or someone. The thoughts raced about in dreadful psychedelic patterns. If I stopped too long it made me feel sick. There was too much going on.

## Always anxious

There was an ever-present darkness that fooled me into believing there was always something to worry about or get anxious over. I never knew what. There was no peace or quiet for my mind. At worst I felt manic and obsessed and at best totally apathetic and agoraphobic. I was unwilling to face the outside world, I wanted to stay safe and contained within my small domestic world.

## Highs and lows

I struggled to deal with overwhelming emotions – sheer extremities. Sometimes I experienced unbelievable 'highs'. I would wake up and feel my mania with the first waking breaths. The day would be a whirl of getting things done and controlling my world – everything in it becoming ordered and perfect. I was exhilarated, imagining that I had overthrown 'the enemy' at last.

Invariably, I would bounce back down to earth with a ferocity that crushed me. I hit the depths again, feeling that I was worse than ever and I'd reached the final onset of a madness that would never end.

'I'd found a place where we could share our lives, anguish and deepest fears. Relief flooded my mind. I had discovered a sisterhood; they all spoke a language that I understood. Every story contained echoes of my life, it was a revelation.'

Rose's group was invaluable, reminding me of things that my fevered mind found it hard to hang on to – this would end and I would never be as ill as I was in the beginning. I must ride it through.

## Who am I today?

The up and down phenomenon was one of the most trying aspects of the illness. Manic 'happiness' left me exhausted and shattered. The low that followed was even harder to bear. The extreme outpouring of feelings that followed was usually a tempest of bitter and prolonged crying. My face and eyes could be swollen and red for days.

The cycle produced the Jekyll and Hyde effect. Who was I today? I would question as I tried to get out of bed. Monster or nice person? It confused me, how would it affect my husband and child? Was I a fraud as well as a madwoman? Was I well or was I ill? Had I imagined it all? Was I just not coping? Was I just a bad mother pretending to have postnatal depression so I could explain all my inadequacies and laziness away? There were many false starts – so many promises of recovery and I was knocked back each time. How would I really know when the beginning of the end of this roller coaster illness came?

## Putting on an act

I became an Oscar-winning actress. My friends didn't know a thing. You always seemed to smile, they say now. I have heard this referred to as the 'smiling illness'. It's a time of your life when you are supposed to smile. The extra pressure and pain of the emotional anguish forces one of the brightest, happiest smiles onto your face.

## You will get better

Today, the smile on my face is real and heartfelt. The strangest thing of all is that I don't regret a moment of my illness. It turned me into the new and improved person I am today.

'Manic "happiness" left me exhausted and shattered. The low that followed was even harder to bear. The extreme outpouring of feelings that followed was usually a tempest of bitter and prolonged crying.'

I am stronger. I appreciate my happiness, family and health more. The small things in life really seem to count. Petty things and attitudes have been put into their proper places. I love my husband and daughter even more and I have a beautiful son now. I have much more to offer my children and I am a better mother than I would have been. I understand how strong I am. I have a deep faith in other people – the experience they share with you and the promises they make is a valuable and worthwhile thing.

The illness has given me a new perspective and enriched life in ways too numerous and subtle to list. Each day brings a new revelation. It is as if I have finally woken up, but I have woken up as a new person with a better life.

'The illness has given me a new perspective and has enriched life in ways too numerous and subtle to list. Each day brings a new revelation. It is as if I have finally woken up, but I have woken up as a new person with a better life.'

# Summing Up

- The turning point in my recovery was involving someone outside the home. In our case, it was the health visitor who recognised postnatal depression immediately.

- When we knew what we were up against, we could start to tackle the condition. We approached postnatal depression from every angle – antidepressants, group therapy and good old-fashioned teamwork. My recovery was full of extreme highs and equally extreme lows.

- At the end of the nightmare, things have never been better. I am a better person and we are a stronger family as a result. Would I change anything? No, every experience, good and bad, gives you something that makes you the person you are today.

# Chapter Three

# Causes of Postnatal Depression

You've just had a baby and feel more vulnerable than you've ever felt before. Then you get postnatal depression. Assuming you manage to identify why you are feeling the way you do, the next thing you want to know is, why? Why have you been hit with this devastating condition when you should be enjoying and celebrating life with a new baby in your arms?

## What did I do to deserve this?

The first thing that a new mother needs to understand is that postnatal depression is indiscriminate; it strikes right through society and was first identified hundreds of years ago. Many studies have concluded that as many as 13% of new mothers suffer from postnatal depression (O'Hara and Swain, 1996).

Postnatal depression is not personal. You didn't deserve to get ill and you haven't brought this on yourself. To get better, it's really important you accept this. If you understand and get to know postnatal depression, it feels less frightening and controlling.

Many ideas and theories about the triggers of postnatal depression have been examined over the years. There has never been a definitive answer to the cause but most modern theories fall into three distinct categories:

- Biological factors.
- Psychological factors.
- Social factors.

'Postnatal depression is not personal. You didn't deserve to get ill and you haven't brought this on yourself. To get better, it's really important you accept this. If you understand and get to know postnatal depression, it feels less frightening and controlling.'

The only thing that most experts have agreed on is that the most likely explanation is that postnatal depression occurs when there is a tendency to develop postnatal illness. This combines with other factors to increase your likelihood of falling ill.

# Biological factors

The biological explanation of postnatal depression hinges on hormonal activities during a time of massive changes.

During pregnancy, the levels of oestrogen and progesterone rise at a rate that is unmatched at any other time in a woman's life. Following the birth of her baby, the opposite effect is experienced with consequences which can tip the emotional balance.

## Puerperal psychosis

Puerperal psychosis is thought to be wholly caused by the effect of hormonal changes. It's an extreme form of postnatal depression which often results in a woman being admitted to hospital. The symptoms are frightening and include hallucinations and severe delusions. It is a very distinct illness and shouldn't be confused with postnatal depression.

## The baby blues

The baby blues are thought to be wholly attributable to hormones. This is also a very distinct condition from postnatal depression. Some people who claim they have experienced postnatal depression have experienced nothing more than the baby blues.

It occurs three or four days after the baby's birth and often coincides with the onset of the milk supply. You feel tearful, sad and perhaps unable to cope for a few days. A full recovery is made very quickly.

'The baby blues are thought to be wholly attributable to hormones. This is also a very distinct condition from postnatal depression.'

## Thyroid disease

Thyroid disease is a common effect of pregnancy. It frequently occurs within the months following childbirth and often remains unidentified. With profound symptoms which include extreme fatigue, weight change and depression, thyroid disease is sometimes overlooked by GPs and diagnosed as an incidence of postnatal depression. Bear this in mind and ask for your thyroid levels to be tested with a simple blood test.

# Psychological factors

Psychological causes of postnatal depression can be just as powerful and overwhelming as physical explanations. They should never be overlooked. Think about whether any of these apply to you.

## Previous history of mental health

A previous history of mental health includes conditions such as bipolar disorder, an earlier incidence of postnatal depression or anxiety disorders.

## Depressed during pregnancy

Not all women find their pregnancy a joy. For some, there is a deep sense of anxiety or sadness. It's unsettling and often goes unrecorded because it's just not 'natural'. Just be aware that if you experienced any of these feelings during pregnancy, it can contribute to postnatal illness.

## Family history of postnatal depression

Ask questions, you will be very surprised how many people come forward and tell you they have experienced postnatal depression. When it's a close relative like a mother, sister, grandmother or aunt, your condition may start to make more sense. The tendency to contract postnatal depression is much stronger if there is a family history.

'Not all women find their pregnancy a joy. For some, there is a deep sense of anxiety or sadness.'

## Are there specific personality types who suffer?

If you have unrealistic expectations of parenthood you are more at risk of postnatal depression. You'll find it harder to adjust to motherhood. Babies aren't born with timetables or agendas and, for the first time, you have to adjust to placing your needs in a position far behind those of your baby's. The huge changes that need to be addressed can't be understated. Habits and personality traits are built up through a lifetime. They are challenged and stretched within moments of a baby's birth and for the rest of your lifetime.

# Social factors

'Babies aren't born with timetables or agendas and, for the first time, you have to adjust to placing your needs in a position far behind those of your baby's.'

No woman is an island and the way in which you fit into society makes a big difference to your personal and emotional health as a new mother.

## Home life

A disruptive marital or home life is very likely to trigger postnatal depression. It adds extra pressure to a woman's emotions when stability and security are of key importance.

Postnatal depression has increased at a time when social and family structures are splintered and daughters are likely to live some distance from the support and care of mothers, aunts and sisters. It means that you will usually be sole carer and it doesn't allow you the possibility of offloading your emotions and concerns with people you feel safe with. Gone are the days when you could knock on the door down the street and have someone who cares come to your rescue at a moment's notice.

## Health issues

Taking care of a new baby is tough at any time, but if your physical health isn't up to scratch, it's even harder.

Some mothers have pre-existing health conditions which add extra challenges to motherhood. Giving birth often leaves behind war wounds, like stitches from a caesarean delivery, you are bound to feel some discomfort as a result.

Having a baby is an incredibly demanding process which leaves you feeling physically exhausted. There is rarely time to recover full strength and sleep quotas, which means that a new mother is often more vulnerable and prone to illnesses like postnatal depression.

## Traumatic birth

A traumatic birth can create feelings of anxiety and fear resulting in post-traumatic stress disorder. Increased levels of medical supervision and poor aftercare raise the possibility of trauma. It's another reason to mourn the lost days when women felt safe and secure giving birth within the familiar realms of their own bedroom.

## Babies who aren't well

A sick baby increases your chances of developing postnatal depression. This arises from feelings of failure to protect your child and a sense of self-blame. While they are very real emotions, they are completely unfounded.

# The importance of the causes

It's important to know and understand the causes of postnatal depression; if you stand back from the condition and treat it as something that has 'come' to you and isn't part of you, you can begin to see a way to deal with it.

Looking at the causes of the illness identifies areas that apply to you. It's about piecing your story together like a jigsaw. There is an explanation and a cause. A cause means your illness has a beginning and reaffirms that it will end.

'Increased levels of medical supervision and poor aftercare raise the possibility of trauma. It's another reason to mourn the lost days when women felt safe and secure giving birth within the familiar realms of their own bedroom.'

# Summing Up

- You can't blame yourself for getting postnatal depression. In fact, self-blame is more likely to make things worse. Postnatal depression happens to women of any child-bearing age, background or culture. It is a worldwide phenomenon. The only criterion is to have a baby!

- Nobody knows what causes postnatal depression but the main areas have been identified which hold the keys to why the illness strikes. These are biological, psychological and social factors.

- Never underestimate the powerful effects hormones have on your wellbeing. They are prime suspects as causes for the distinctly separate conditions of the baby blues and puerperal psychosis. Both illnesses illustrate the relationship between mental wellbeing and physical processes. Consider the possibility of thyroid disease which is frequently confused with postnatal depression.

- These key areas identify the women who are more vulnerable to develop postnatal depression. It doesn't mean they are guaranteed to contract the illness. The most likely scenario is that a whole combination of factors across the three key areas work together to create a situation where postnatal depression is more likely to occur.

- Understanding some of the causes of postnatal depression is useful because it helps to distance the illness from the sufferer.

- A cause denotes a beginning and if there's a beginning, there's also an end. The probable causes of postnatal depression give the sufferer valuable clues about how to approach their illness and ideas to help deal with daily life.

'If you stand back from the condition and treat it as something that has "come" to you and isn't part of you, you can begin to see a way to deal with it.'

# Chapter Four

# The Signs and Symptoms

If you've got postnatal depression, it's easy to diagnose, you get depressed and sad. Right? Wrong. The difficulty with postnatal depression is that it causes a whole host of symptoms.

Everyone suffers a different combination of symptoms and two cases are never the same. Often you will be oblivious to the changes in your behaviour. You may have a sense that 'something isn't right' but it's really tough to step back and assess whether you are suffering with this illness or not. This is where the people who surround you are so important. They have an objective view and find it easier to spot tell-tale signs and symptoms that all is not well.

## Look for the signs

It's important to identify the illness sooner rather than later. Recognising the illness early means you can deal with the situation head on and channel energy into treating the condition rather than wondering what on earth is happening.

You don't have to suffer with all the 'common' symptoms to suffer from postnatal depression. Only a few might be present, in any combination or varying degrees of severity.

If you have any real concerns – begin keeping a 'mood' diary. This is a simple daily list of any moods, thoughts or behaviours that worry you. It can be an important tool to help you highlight things that just don't feel right.

'You may have a sense that "something isn't right" but it's really tough to step back and assess whether you are suffering with this illness or not. This is where the people who surround you are so important.'

## Depression

This is the most obvious sign to look out for, but it's an umbrella term which manifests itself in lots of different ways. The simplest definition is that it means you feel sad. You can be sad all the time or some of the time.

Often people exhibiting depressive moods experience periods of deep lows and extreme highs. It can be incredibly confusing when you think that you might be depressed. The key to recognising this trait is that the high is unnatural, unsustainable and leaves you feeling exhausted. Other depressive symptoms might include:

'There is a powerful sense of mental and emotional fatigue. You experience an extreme lack of energy which leaves you with very little enthusiasm for anything in life.'

- Feeling that you are living in a world or life totally without hope.

- Feeling tearful – the tears might always feel like they're just below the surface ready to roll down your cheeks at a moment's notice or without any warning.

- Blaming yourself for things that are beyond your control – you might feel responsible for any misfortune or wrongdoing you hear of.

- Feeling insecure – suddenly you are unsure of your place in the world, your role or whether you even deserve to have a life and feature in the lives of those around you.

## Tiredness

The sort of tiredness experienced by mothers suffering with postnatal depression is quite different from that experienced by all new mothers. It's more persistent and is not relieved by regular sleeps or naps. There is a powerful sense of mental and emotional fatigue. You experience an extreme lack of energy which leaves you with very little enthusiasm for anything in life. You become very apathetic and even the tiniest task, such as brushing your teeth can feel like a monumental challenge.

Sometimes the lethargy is confused with genuine physical tiredness and there is a danger you will withdraw from daily life to the safety and sanctuary of your bed. This is fine every now and then, but can be dangerous and counter-productive on a regular basis.

Tiredness is often tied up with sleep disturbances that create a vicious circle. Elements of insomnia creep in, exaggerated by the topsy-turvy hours of feeding a new baby throughout the night. The need to catch up on sleep during the day and a troubled emotional state all work together to cause varying levels of sleep disturbance.

## Isolation and withdrawal

Isolation and withdrawal are common responses to the way you are feeling. You may feel unworthy of being a part of a family or various social circles and it seems easier to withdraw altogether.

You might feel that security lies within the four walls of home and is preferable to facing the challenges and threats posed by the outside world. Unfortunately, this tends to cause a downward spiral as social confidence and new experiences are restricted, feelings of depression are deepened and intensified.

## Anxiety

Constant feelings of anxiety cause a great deal of distress. Anxiety has nothing to do with your feeling that things aren't going to plan.

The real definition of anxiety is a constant and invasive feeling that something dreadful will happen to you, your baby or a loved one. It's an ever-present black cloud that colours every decision, action or thought you have.

Anxiety causes unwelcome thoughts which question the safety of you, your child or your family. You may believe you are a bad mother and a bad person with no control over the world around you.

Anxiety doesn't come alone and often brings panic attacks into your life. These are extremely disturbing incidents that make you feel intensely frightened, short of breath, out of control and fearful for your life. Panic attack sufferers often claim that an attack feels like they are fighting for every breath.

'The real definition of anxiety is a constant and invasive feeling that something dreadful will happen to you, your baby or a loved one. It's an ever-present black cloud that colours every decision, action or thought you have.'

## Obsessive behaviours and changed thoughts

Unusual behaviours are spotted more easily by the people surrounding you than yourself. Thoughts tend to repeat themselves over and over until you believe they are the truth. The thoughts centre on dark feelings about yourself, your baby and the world around you.

A lot of new mothers are disturbed that, at a time when they are surrounded by new life and birth, they increasingly worry about death, dying and illness. Some people become convinced that the emotional effects they are experiencing relate to a physical illness that will result in death. This makes feelings of hopelessness more sinister and it becomes increasingly difficult to see the beautiful and joyful things that life has to offer.

'Family and friends need to be aware that some behaviours or changes to mood could be attributed to the possibility of substance abuse.'

Sometimes, you might feel compelled to punish or harm yourself – it's a way of gaining some control over your life and emotions. Carers and family might notice that you develop obsessive routines or behaviours. This might be related to diet or ways in which you pass your time – perhaps extreme cleaning or shopping. These behaviour patterns chase feelings of satisfaction and contentment. It's a way of trying to gain control over life and feelings. The effect of the behaviour is very short-lived and the actions are repeated until they become obsessive.

These behaviours are very similar to a common condition called obsessive compulsive disorder (OCD). They are more difficult to deal with when mixed up with postnatal depression, as there is also a baby to consider. A lot of mums may be seen to be taking motherhood to new extremes, by worrying that the slightest deviation from the routine they think is best will cause serious harm to the baby, or will show them up to be the bad mother they think they are. Typical concerns that become obsessive are whether they can keep the baby clean enough, provide a hygienic home and nursery, or feed the baby so just the right amount of weight goes on each week.

Obsessive behaviour and emotions could result in substance abuse of alcohol, food, prescription drugs or even illegal substances. Family and friends need to be aware that some behaviours or changes to mood could be attributed to the possibility of substance abuse.

## The inability to bond with your baby

The inability to bond with your baby is a very distressing and troubling effect of postnatal depression. It comes at a time when you are supposed to be at your most maternal. The difficulties in forging a deep relationship with your baby feels like a terrible failure and makes you feel unnatural and monstrous. The baby might feel alien and frighten you. This is noticeable in situations required to make close contact with the baby, like when they cry, need feeding or changing. Mothers in this situation are dependent on other people to care for the baby and feel dreadfully ashamed by their emotions.

# Summing Up

- Many symptoms of postnatal depression can be missed or misinterpreted. It's very hard for new mums to see themselves as others do, so it's really helpful if the people closest to you know about some of the signs that indicate postnatal depression.

- Postnatal depression doesn't have a set menu of symptoms. There are lots of different signs that occur in any combination. The quicker the symptoms are identified, the better. Energy can then be directed towards supporting you.

- Some of the symptoms to look out for include classic signs of depression, tiredness, the inability to bond with your new baby, isolation and withdrawal, anxiety and changed or obsessive behaviour.

- Above all, stay alert and try to identify and interpret the signs as soon as the issues become apparent.

# Chapter Five

# The First Stop for Help

Postnatal depression can make you feel detached from the world or reality. It feels like you're living in a bubble by yourself. A lot of sufferers say their lives become unreal and they begin to question their thoughts constantly.

This is why it's important to be properly assessed and diagnosed at the earliest opportunity. Getting a firm diagnosis validates how you're feeling and marks the first stop on your road to recovery. It's impossible to start getting better until you know what you're dealing with.

## Friends and family

Usually close family and friends are experts at spotting problems with loved ones but it's not that straightforward with postnatal illnesses. Many new mums are guilty about negative emotions associated with the birth of a baby and they will go to great lengths to hide, dismiss or lessen the issues they are trying to cope with.

It's a good idea to plan in advance. Make sure your partner or closest friends are well-versed in the clues that point to this illness.

Honesty and openness is absolutely key. It's very hard to open your mouth for the first time, but you must ask for help. Tell at least one person you can trust so the ball of recovery can start rolling. The sooner it starts to roll, the sooner the momentum will pick up and you will feel much better much quicker.

# Why hide it?

There is no place for pride here. It takes a brave woman to speak up and let someone know she is having difficulties and may be experiencing postnatal depression. Imagine you broke your wrist and couldn't write or perform daily chores and activities, would you try to hide your situation? Or would you tell someone who could help you get through your day and make sure you received the appropriate treatment? One is a physical difficulty and the other mental. Why would you treat one differently from the other?

Speak out – it's the most important thing you can do to help yourself.

'It takes a brave woman to speak up and let someone know she is having difficulties and may be experiencing postnatal depression.'

## Health visitors

Every new mother is assigned a health visitor allocated to her following the birth of a new baby. As the midwife steps away from her duties, those of the health visitor begin. This is usually around 10 days or so after the birth of the baby.

During their visits, the health visitor checks the baby's progress and records the information for the child's personal health records

She should also ask an important question during her time with you, 'How are you feeling?' This is a golden opportunity for you to let her know exactly how you are. Telling the health visitor that things aren't well isn't shameful or a reason to feel you have failed. Remember the principles of the broken wrist? It's no different, keep telling yourself that over and over.

People fear that by telling the health visitor you have difficulties with your mental wellbeing is risking your reputation as a good mother. They worry their babies will be taken away or they'll be reported to the authorities. These are unfounded fears that are part of the illness you are experiencing. No such thing will happen and the health visitor just wants to start making plans for your care and recovery.

# How can my GP help?

If, for some reason, you haven't informed your health visitor, make an appointment to see your GP.

If you can't relate to your GP, it's usually possible to see another member of the practice. You might like to take someone to your appointment for support. Often it's a bit of a blur and it helps to have someone at your side.

Think about the things you want to tell the GP and make a small 'prompt' list about some of the symptoms bothering you. If you are having a 'foggy' day, it can be really tough to keep your thinking clear, so write it all down.

Don't worry about getting upset. Take a look at any GP's desk and there's always a little box of tissues. They are there for a reason; you will be one in a long line to reach for them.

However tough your visit might feel, it's the first huge step towards getting better.

# Other sources of information

Arming yourself with information is the most effective and powerful way to start dealing with postnatal depression. We are one of the luckiest generations that have ever dealt with this illness. For the first time, all the information and a wealth of personal anecdotes and advice is in the public domain and it's all waiting there to help you on your journey through this condition.

Dedicated books are being published on the subject. Postnatal depression was often confined to a short paragraph or an information box, but we are fortunate that it has been sufficiently recognised now to merit its own book.

The Internet is a fabulous source of information with many respected health bodies and specialist associations having their own online libraries and resources. This gives you and your family instant, free access to a wealth of information.

'For the first time, all the information and a wealth of personal anecdotes and advice is in the public domain and it's all waiting there to help you on your journey through this condition.'

# Summing Up

- Getting help is the first step on the road to recovery. Sharing your experiences, worries and concerns with third parties makes the situation real and allows you to deal with the situation more effectively.

- Start by speaking to friends and family, the people closest to you. This is a time for honesty and openness. Pride will bring you nothing more than further pressure and continued stress. By sharing your feelings with those closest to you, you will help yourself and make their lives easier too.

- Health visitors are your main source of professional contact after your baby is born. They have a duty of care to mothers as well as their babies. Health visitors are approachable and caring.

- Visiting your GP is another huge step towards receiving the treatment you need. They will be able to explain a whole range of treatment choices and plans to you.

- Above all, get help as soon as you are able. Your journey to recovery needs to get going as early as possible.

# Chapter Six

# Helping Yourself

We've all heard the expression, 'life goes on'. This is so true after the birth of a baby but never tougher to follow through if you're suffering with postnatal depression.

## Life goes on

Just when you want to curl up in a ball and make everything come to a halt, there's a new mouth to feed, laundry piling up and, in some cases, older siblings to ferry to school. Nobody thinks to cancel Christmas, birthdays, Easter, sports days or social events – life goes on and somehow you are expected to cope. There are some tricks and tips that will help you through your life with postnatal depression, tricks to make life easier to deal with and help you to help yourself.

There isn't a golden rule. The best approach to life is a mixed approach. Not all the ideas will work for you but you can try them out and find out what's best for your circumstances.

## Turning to words

It sounds like an odd concept – using words to help you through your troubles. This feels like the worst time of your life, why would you want to record any part of it? Writing things down and documenting your experience is incredibly valuable for so many reasons. You don't have to be a modern-day Shakespeare and it doesn't matter if what you write is nonsense. It is an opportunity to make all the things going on deep inside your mind leap onto paper – instantly relieving some of the pressure that is building up inside you.

'Just when you want to curl up in a ball and make everything come to a halt, there's a new mouth to feed, laundry piling up and, in some cases, older siblings to ferry to school.'

Recovery from postnatal depression is usually very gradual. It's often so slow it's hard to tell how you are doing. Keeping a diary is a simple and concrete way to see the improvements.

Try jotting down a few words at the end of each day. All you need is five minutes with your thoughts and feelings. When you have something on paper, mark the day in your diary, for example, if it has been a 'bad' day, make a red dot, an average day use blue and a really good day could be a smiley face.

Just by flicking through your diary every now and then, you will be amazed to see how you have changed throughout the months. It's quite normal to have a huge dip in your mood when you feel you have been making good progress. By picking up the diary, you can reassure yourself that this is a blip which is a small part of a much larger upward trend.

'A traumatised mum feels as though she is "stuck" at the birth and unable to move on emotionally. This is where it's so useful to write it down. Write the story of the birth from start to finish.'

## Getting it out of your system

Sometimes, new mums believe the reason they are depressed is due to the events surrounding their baby's birth. Symptoms of postnatal depression are very similar to those of post-traumatic stress disorder.

Society is fond of reminding us that childbirth is the proudest and most amazing moment of a woman's life, but we are quick to overlook that it can be the most destructive and traumatic time of her life too. A traumatised mum feels as though she is 'stuck' at the birth and unable to move on emotionally. This is where it's so useful to write it down.

Write the story of the birth from start to finish, detailing your feelings and deepest emotions and fears. When you have completed your story, there are two options. Either pass a copy of it to someone close so they can share the depths of your feelings. If this isn't for you, seal the document in an envelope, date it and put it away somewhere safe. It may never see daylight again. That doesn't matter. Your experience has been recorded and your feelings have been translated to words on paper, all of which should make you feel relieved of your lonely burden.

# Learn to share

Emotional turmoil is magnified and intensified if it's kept hidden away. Learning to share your thoughts and experiences is a big step forward. Sharing is a two-way process which enables you to collect wisdom and new perspectives from other people too.

## Friends and family

Talking is probably the most valuable tool you can use to help you recover. Talk to partners, family and friends. There's no reason why you should keep this illness to yourself. If you broke your arm, there would be no secrecy or shame. Ask yourself why suffering with postnatal depression should be any different.

Talking about how you're feeling and sharing your experiences will allow you to accept help, new ideas and fresh opinions. For many people, it's the first step towards accepting their illness and making plans for getting better.

## Support groups

Share your experience with a support group. The last thing you need is to feel isolated. Surrounding yourself with people who are suffering with the same illness, normalises you and helps you realise your feelings aren't unusual or odd. It's another step forward to accepting postnatal depression as part of your life and learning to live through it.

Most health visitors have access to a range of support groups in your area. You often find details at libraries and doctors' surgeries or health centres. If you have any problems finding information, you will always uncover something with a quick Internet search. Specialised parenting websites are a particularly good source of advice.

'Surrounding yourself with people who are suffering with the same illness, normalises you and helps you realise your feelings aren't unusual or odd.'

## Delegating

By letting other people know how you are feeling you allow them to become part of your emotional journey. They will hopefully want to help and may offer a hand with daily chores and duties.

Delegating is a skill and it's a learned behaviour which feels alien to a lot of people. Recognise the learning process and when it's right to hand over parts of your life to other people.

You are developing your character and allowing people who care for you to feel valued and helpful. Delegating prevents other people around you from feeling excluded from your life.

# Recognise the journey

Some of the language people use when they talk about how to deal with postnatal depression is very interesting. They talk about 'battling', 'fighting' or 'wrestling' with the condition. Setting yourself up for a fight seems to suggest you can win or lose. If you hit a bad patch, it's too easy to give up on a losing battle.

Accept you have postnatal depression and visualise yourself at one end of a train track. Lying in front of you is a journey. There are ups and downs, mountain tops and dark valleys, potholes, tunnels and beautiful views. You can't be sure of the exact route but you will be in a different place at your journey's end. It's up to you to make the destination a better place than your point of departure. As you make your journey keep some important truths locked in your mind.

## Why aren't I perfect?

There's no need to be perfect, it's bound to drag you down. This is a time of life that is imagined to be surrounded by the rosy glow of motherhood with a neat home filled with the smell of home-made cooking and warm, clean babies.

That image isn't real life and the truth is that your journey with postnatal depression is the ideal time to gently lower your expectations. No mother is perfect (and if they are, they're not being 100% truthful!) You are allowed to be 'good enough' and no more. If you are unable to breastfeed, you can bottle-feed instead and that is good enough. If you don't feel well enough to go to the baby signing, baby music and baby massage classes that's fine too, you are good enough. Make this your motto.

## Celebrate the changes

Perhaps you feel postnatal depression has changed your personality and you will never be the same again. This is true, but you will be stronger and improved. If some of the behaviours, thoughts and feelings you experience seem alien to you, that's exactly what they are.

## Why can't I be like ...?

Remember over and over that comparing yourself to other people is a fruitless exercise. It leaves you feeling inadequate. Human nature is great at marking other people's qualities up while you judge yourself so badly.

## Will this ever end?

All journeys have a beginning and an end. If there's one thought that needs to roll over endlessly in your head during the darkest days, it's 'this will end'.

It would be a great time to trot out the clichés like 'the light at the end of the tunnel' or the 'lowest ebb is the turn of the tide' but let's look at why they are clichés. It's because they are age-old truths, things that everyone should know, but are so easily forgotten. Say it over and over, write it down and put it on the fridge, do whatever it takes to make this phrase a part of your life – 'this will end'.

'All journeys have a beginning and an end. If there's one thought that needs to roll over endlessly in your head during the darkest days, it's "this will end".'

# Be your own boss

Life feels difficult enough, so stick to a couple of basic principles. Make sure you know what's going on in your mind, understand what's happening and keep life clear, simple and planned. You'll feel more in control and life will be improved.

## How can I make life simpler?

If you are anxious about certain situations, try to avoid them. Do you really need to worry about the baby bawling non-stop when you get on the bus? Ask someone else to get your shopping, order online or take a walk to the shops in the fresh air instead. Why are you worrying about holding back the tears when you meet up with all your friends tonight? Ask yourself if big social situations are right for you at the moment. If it all feels a bit much, invite one or two friends over for a takeaway instead or postpone until you are feeling stronger.

Don't pack your diary, instead learn to say no to commitments and duties that cloud or complicate your life. Plan your life around your feelings and insulate yourself against your fears so at least some of the stress disappears.

## Learn all about it

Life is much easier if you are in the know – so educate and inform yourself. Look out for information about postnatal depression.

A word of caution though, you can over research. The Internet is full of forums and chat rooms where mums suffering with postnatal depression swap stories and ideas. People tend to write volumes about their bad days and very little about the good. It can paint a very imbalanced view of life with postnatal depression.

Focus on arming yourself with facts about the illness, coping tactics that you feel work for you and a plan for recovery. Personal anecdotes are very useful to help you feel 'normal' but daily updates of other people's problems can drag you right back down into the darkness.

## Plan your life

If life feels too chaotic, this is the time to try action plans and timetables in your life. This doesn't have to be strict and regimented but it helps to clear your thoughts if you can keep life simple and transparent.

Wall planners and lists are wonderful tools in the right hands. Don't aim to be perfectly organised, just enough to keep life ticking over at a 'good' and simple level.

Targets and goals can be great for motivating you when there is little drive or energy left. Stick to simple goals like making sure you and the baby are dressed before midday, for example. That's good enough for now.

'Don't aim to be perfectly organised, just enough to keep life ticking over at a "good" and simple level. Targets and goals are great for motivating you when there is little drive or energy left.'

# Summing Up

- The 'helping yourself' approach is not the same as 'pulling yourself together' or 'getting on with it'. It's a plan to help you take charge of your recovery and the way you deal with life, even the darkest days. The plan should take the form of several different approaches, all working together to create a safety net for you.

- Start writing your thoughts and experiences down in diaries or journals. It helps to clear your head and chart your recovery. You can read about the good days on the bad days.

- Share your life with other people. Talk, talk, talk and talk again. Talk to friends, relatives, other sufferers – anyone who wants to listen. Try to find a support group, this is invaluable therapy.

- Learn to delegate and share your life with others who can help you or shoulder some of your responsibilities when you are feeling unwell.

- Accept your journey as part of life. For now, you don't need to be a perfect wife, girlfriend, mother, friend or employee. Accept you are good enough. Don't compare yourself with anyone and remember this is a passing phase of your life. It is a journey with a destination. This will end.

- Plan your life and avoid stress as far as you can. Use gentle targets and timetables to give your life some structure and shape. Make sure you read and educate yourself – things are much easier to deal with when you know what you are up against.

# Chapter Seven

# Taking Care

The last thing a new mum should do is to forget to take care of herself. Unfortunately postnatal depression is good at clouding your judgement and people often ignore the neglect and lack of care they are heaping on themselves.

## The inner you

If you can't look after the woman that looks back at you in the mirror every morning, try turning your attention to the inner you. It seems like an odd idea but if you can trust this suggestion, it works wonders.

Make a start by imagining your 'inner you'. Some people find this easier by picturing this as a child or a small furry animal that needs nurturing. Keep the 'new' inner you in mind at all times.

If it helps, draw a picture or choose a picture from a magazine that appeals to your caring nature, cut it out and keep it next to your bed. Look at it first thing in the morning and last thing at night. Focus your caring energies onto this vulnerable inner you.

## Proper food

To function properly you need a good diet. Forget counting calories and making radical changes to the food you enjoy. Just think about the fuel you expect your body and mind to survive on.

'Forget counting calories and making radical changes to the food you enjoy. Just think about the fuel you expect your body and mind to survive on.'

A good, balanced diet will maintain a healthy immune system and make you feel better all round. The trick is to eat a diet that contains plenty of freshly prepared food including fruit and vegetables, protein and energy-giving carbohydrates.

It's really important that you eat small meals regularly rather than having long stretches of the day when you are famished followed by blow-out feasts. This helps maintain the right blood sugar levels which will assist with your energy levels and stop unsettling mood swings.

When suffering from depression, people are hardwired to crave the food that gives instant comfort. Typical foods to turn to are:

- Chocolate.
- Cakes.
- Crisps.
- Wine.
- Chips.
- Fast food.

These junk foods seem like a great fix at the time but they usually work against you in the end. The feel-good effects are temporary and you start to feel guilty for eating 'bad' foods or bingeing. They do nothing to make you feel better about yourself.

## How can I eat a healthier diet?

It's fine to eat the food on the 'bad' list but make sure you have specific times when you eat them, such as a chocolate bar at the weekend. You won't feel deprived and no one could accuse you of eating badly if you enjoy healthy meals the rest of the time.

Plan your meals and snacks if you can and think of new ways to keep your food healthy.

- For an instant sugar hit try a handful of super-sweet juicy raisins.

- If nothing but chocolate will do, try a mug of low-fat hot chocolate drink to chase the cravings away.

- Thinking of fast food? Think of pasta with a tomato-based sauce.

# Keep on moving

When it's an effort to get out of bed in the morning, it's a huge leap to consider taking any exercise. Most people experience a 'high' after exercise, it's thought that exercise helps to release hormones called endorphins that raise your mood and emotional wellbeing which will be really beneficial if you're suffering from postnatal depression.

Be gentle but remind yourself that even if you don't like the idea of exercise, it's still worth giving it a go. There is something out there for everyone – so do some research and think about ways of moving that you'll enjoy, it could be swimming or yoga for relaxing physical activities. Try running if you want to get rid of some frustration that's built up inside you, or walking to get out in the open air and appreciate the environment – anything you like really.

If you're worried that you will talk yourself out of any exercise, think about finding an exercise buddy. It'll be much harder to skive and it's a chance to talk, which is always excellent therapy.

# Rest and relaxation

Sleep is a big problem for a lot of postnatal depression sufferers, too much sleeping, not enough or a mixture of both.

Sleep hygiene has nothing to do with spring-cleaning the bedroom, it helps create and plan a good going-to-bed routine. Most mothers have one in place for their babies but forget to think of themselves.

Here are some ideas to create a sleep hygiene routine for yourself and hopefully it will go some way to helping you regain healthy sleeping habits:

- Keep your bedroom as a place to sleep – not to eat, watch TV, study or sort laundry.

'Sleep hygiene has nothing to do with spring-cleaning the bedroom, it helps create and plan a good going-to-bed routine.'

- Think about the temperature of your room – is it too warm? Could a window be opened? Perhaps the room is too cold?

- Try to go to bed at a set time – neither too late nor too early and get up at the same time every day. After a refreshing night's sleep, note down your sleep times and try the same hours again the following night. Sometimes it takes a while to find your ideal 'sleep cycle' but it's worth the effort.

- Don't oversleep – this is really tempting when you're depressed. It's a good way to escape from the turmoil but as a long-term strategy it won't help at all.

## Take comfort

'Don't squander the time doing nothing or watching endless TV programmes, stay mindful and care for yourself.'

This is the ideal time to lavish attention onto yourself but it's the time we are most unlikely to do so. You need to be 'mindful' at all times. Find ways to remind yourself over and over that you need care and nurturing. Even if you have to mark it in your diary or write it in huge red letters on your fridge, you have to make time for yourself.

Don't squander your comfort time doing nothing or watching endless TV programmes, stay mindful and care for yourself. These are times of escapism. They are little snatches of time when you can take yourself away from where you are emotionally and immerse yourself in activities which offer you satisfaction, pleasure and contentment.

Try some different comforting activities out and see what makes you feel the most comfortable and cosy:

- Read a good book – something easy-to-read but engaging.

- Wallow in a long, hot bath with oils and candlelight

- Enjoy a film – something uplifting, a comedy, a fantasy, an old classic – whatever suits your taste.

- Leaf through a magazine and daydream.

- Take up a craft or hobby, either something new or an old favourite.

46

If you are weighed down by low moods, it can be difficult to come up with anything you enjoy or gives you pleasure. A great tip is to make a 'feel-good list'.

Jot down all the things you've done or would like to do that would make you happy and why. Keep your list safe and when you are feel low, but mindful that you need some time to yourself, refer to your special list and pick something you can try. Don't worry if once you've started your activity, you can't continue, stop or move down the list and see if you can pick something else out.

## Create a comfort zone

Children and babies depend on comforters for security and reassurance. It's a lesson for mums too. You may already have a comfort zone without consciously knowing that's what it is, or you may need to find one that will help you through your postnatal depression. Your comfort zone could be:

- A favourite chair.
- A throw or rug you like to curl up under.
- A favourite picture that brings you peace.
- A room that brings you a feeling of cosiness.
- A piece of music to soothe your mind.
- Books of poetry or proverbs that focus and calm your thoughts.

# Summing Up

- Taking care of others should never stop you from taking care of yourself. Picture an alternative 'inner you' as a focus for you to love and cherish.

- Make sure you eat healthily to help your body get through the day – try to stay away from too many junk foods.

- Do some gentle exercise to get your endorphins flowing – the thought of doing exercise will probably be really unpleasant, but it will have a great effect on you physically and mentally.

- Try to get into a regular rest and sleep routine – make your bedroom conducive to sleep by not using it for anything other than sleeping.

- Do things and activities that bring you peace and comfort. Take a little bit of 'you' time when you need it and do something you enjoy.

- Paying attention to the 'inner you' will make your road to recovery a much smoother and easier route.

# Chapter Eight

# Coping with Motherhood

You might be worried that your postnatal depression will adversely affect your baby. You are battling some unwelcome feelings and trying to be the best mother possible. The two just don't seem to go together do they? How does postnatal depression affect your baby and how can you make things better for you both?

Having postnatal depression does not make you a bad mother. It's not your fault and accepting all the help and advice available will make you an outstanding mother.

Medical experts believe that if you leave postnatal depression to run its course without treatment at all, there are certain ways your baby might be affected.

■ There may be a sense of detachment between mum and baby as the baby grows and develops.

■ The baby may become a less emotionally secure child.

■ If the baby has little contact with its mother, they might be slower to speak and develop certain life and educational skills.

This should never be used as a basis to blame yourself, don't forget babies have a limited understanding of deep emotions.

## Transferring big feelings on to little people

If you feel emotionally vulnerable or insecure, you tend to transfer your feelings on to other people, for example, your baby. You might imagine that you know how your baby is feeling, for example, they won't stop crying because they're so miserable or have colic because your moods unsettle them. This isn't true – you are transferring feelings onto your baby who knows nothing of your postnatal issues.

A mum who is suffering with postnatal depression might think, 'he's crying like that to teach me a lesson,' or, 'he knows I'm trying to get some rest, why is he being so mean by not settling?' A baby has no concept of spite or meanness. They are just busy being babies and their love for their mum is unconditional. You are in this together and it's a journey you must both travel.

'A baby has no concept of spite or meanness. They are just busy being babies and their love for their mum is unconditional. You are in this together and it's a journey you must both travel.'

## Motherhood

The moment you give birth you are a mother and it's all supposed to come naturally – this is wrong. Giving birth means you are able to reproduce but it doesn't mean you are a natural-born mother. This is a myth passed from generation to generation and causes new mothers no end of stress and guilt.

The first overwhelming rush of all-consuming love and motherly care is just not there sometimes. You might feel empty, vacant and detached from your baby. The love will come but it doesn't have to arrive in a rush with your last contraction, sometimes it gently ebbs into your life like an incoming tide. Before you know it you are as in love with your little one as much as the next mother.

## Do things your way

Being a good parent is about looking after your baby as well as you can. It's not about doing what others want you to do, but doing whatever feels right to you.

- Try to avoid parenting how-to books and websites. They can make you feel insecure and inadequate. There are more opinions out there on how to get your baby to sleep than there are babies ever born! Books and websites are useful for hints and tips but when you are low or vulnerable, they can make matters worse. Do what feels right for you, your child and your circumstances.

- If you make a decision about your baby, be confident and stick to it. You never have to justify yourself to other people.

- Some mothers feel ashamed, embarrassed or inadequate because they can't or prefer not to breastfeed. If you decide it's not for you, stick to your decision. Feel confident about a choice that you have made for your own reasons.

# Make life easy for yourself

Keeping life simple means you can spend more time on you and your baby. You are doing your best to deal with a situation that is far from ideal.

## Start a routine

Get into a routine as soon as possible. Babies love it. They like to know what's coming next – a feed, a nap or a play. You'll find the routine of an ordered life easier to deal with too. It helps to reduce stress and creates a security blanket around you both.

## Sleep when the baby sleeps

'Sleep when baby sleeps' makes great sense for so many reasons. If you are sleep-deprived, as most new mums are, you must make up those hours of rest from somewhere and this is the only way.

It slows you down and raises moods, helping you cope with the things that motherhood throws at you. It's really tempting to snatch that time to dash around with the duster or tackle the pile of ironing. You'll start to live your life like a race against time, working through endless lists while baby sleeps – which will lead to more tiredness and feeling more depressed.

'A day with baby can seem like an uphill struggle. An hour feels like a day and you wonder how you are going to get through an entire week. Take things hour by hour, no more than that.'

## Don't look too far ahead

A day with baby can seem like an uphill struggle. An hour feels like a day and you wonder how you are going to get through an entire week. Take things hour by hour, no more than that. Reduce your life to manageable chunks and you'll feel instantly lifted and more optimistic.

## Just be good enough

Being perfect isn't the ultimate prize of motherhood; the aim is to be 'good enough'. Apply this approach to the care of your baby.

A perfectly turned out baby is dressed top to toe and freshly bathed before midday? No, settle for a clean, fed, happy baby in a babygro at teatime. That's good enough to make you a great mother.

## Be prepared

Have everything to hand before baths, feeds or changes. Make lists even if you don't normally resort to this way of jogging your memory. Lists are great ways to keep your thinking clear and ordered. They help to stop that overwhelming fogginess that's all too common with postnatal depression.

Lists are good but don't over-complicate life with lists of lists. The object is to make life clearer and simpler for you and your baby.

## Take sanctuary

Create a sanctuary for you and your baby. If you feel the need, shut the outside world away. Take the phone off the hook and stick a post-it note on the front door proclaiming, 'do not disturb!'

This is one of those rare times in your lives when it's perfectly normal to go AWOL and disappear into your private nest – just you and baby.

# Sharing your baby's life

A great mother doesn't keep her baby to herself, she learns how to delegate. If you have a break from childcare, the times with your baby become more precious and more focused on the quality of the time together. It allows you to take time to recover and focus on yourself.

Friends and family will always be willing to help. What seems like a daily chore to you is a big source of pleasure to them. Don't be afraid to ask for a little bit of help when you need it.

## Outside help

Consider part-time childcare such as day nursery for a few hours a week. Your baby will benefit from increased social interaction and you'll be refreshed and more dedicated.

## Volunteers and schemes

Look into government or local schemes available for new mothers. These are designed to give your baby the best start in life. The schemes often train volunteers who will spend a few hours each week doing whatever it takes to give mum a break. Home-start is a national institution and an absolute lifeline (see help list).

'A great mother doesn't keep her baby to herself, she learns how to delegate. If you have a break from childcare, the times with baby become more precious and more focused on the quality of your time together.'

# Summing Up

- One of the biggest concerns of mothers with postnatal depression is the effect it has on their babies. Seek help quickly and adverse effects can be avoided or minimised.

- There are many ways to give your baby the best start in life, even if the odds seem to be against you. Start by remembering that being a natural-born mother is nothing more than a myth. Good mothering is a skill. All the emotions that are missing will arrive eventually and they'll be even sweeter for the wait!

- The best way to bring up your baby is your way. If it feels right to you, then it is right.

- Make life as easy as possible for you and your baby. Take the short cuts and direct routes to a simple life and daily routine. An easier life means raised moods. Routine, rest and a sense of security will boost your lives enormously.

- Involve other people in your baby's life – your baby will benefit from the increased social interaction and you will benefit from some rest.

- Postnatal depression won't damage your baby's health and wellbeing, depending on the way you deal with your condition. Take control and make life easier for you both.

# Chapter Nine

# For the People Who Care

The people that love us the most often have the toughest ride. When I was desperately ill after the birth of our first child, someone asked my husband, 'How are you?' He was astounded that someone had remembered to ask him.

Sadly, fathers, in-laws, grandmothers and friends are often neglected during this period. They are loyal and steadfast, ready to pick up the pieces while inside they are crumbling, struggling or bubbling over with questions and doubts about what's going on with their loved one. The people who care are often the forgotten side of postnatal depression so this chapter is aimed at anyone caring for someone who is going through postnatal depression – be you a husband or partner, family member or friend.

You can steer a course through the doldrums of postnatal depression with simple techniques that make you more able to care for the sufferer. You need to look at ways to make your life easier and happier. Caring means looking after yourself too.

## What are you up against?

Ignorance breeds fear – the golden rule for any carer is to acquaint themselves with postnatal depression. You will probably be familiar with some of the main symptoms of the illness, but there may be other more subtle symptoms that you've overlooked.

Certain behaviours are noticeable because they differ from your loved one's normal behaviour and to identify these things as a pattern of illness is incredibly reassuring.

'The ones that love us the most often have the toughest ride. When I was desperately ill after the birth of our first child, someone asked my husband, "How are you?" He was astounded that someone had remembered to ask him.'

Reading this book is a great starting point. Use it as a springboard to other sources of information, such as support groups, websites and specialist organisations.

## How do you deal with it?

Call in the professionals at the earliest opportunity. This is not a betrayal but an act of love. It will propel her and your family towards recovery and normality again. If she has previously resisted medical assistance, ask the GP to reassure her why this step is so important for her and for the baby's wellbeing. Even if she can't accept outside help at first, the mists of depression will clear enough for her to see that it was a valuable and important step to take.

Everyone suffering from postnatal depression is different. It's a single illness complicated by your loved one's unique needs and ways of coping or behaving. Thankfully some ideas apply to most sufferers and will be incredibly helpful for you to remember as you care for her.

'Even if she can't accept outside help at first, the mists of depression will clear enough for her to see that it was a valuable and important step to take.'

### It's not her, it's the condition

Postnatal depression produces quite a bit of difficult behaviour, but remember, it's the symptoms that are difficult not the person. This isn't your loved one being obstructive, stubborn or negative – it's an illness like any other. You wouldn't tell a person with a sprained ankle to 'get on with it' and stop relying on their crutches – try to extend this principle to postnatal depression sufferers.

### This won't last forever

Adopt the same mantra that sufferers should repeat over and over and over, 'You will get better'. Remember that this isn't a full stop in your lives, it's a journey through life which takes a slightly different route to the one you perhaps expected. You will both arrive at the same place together and things will return to normal again.

## The only cure is time

Stop looking for a cure – it just isn't there. All you can do is offer support, comfort, reassurance and security to help your loved one through their postnatal depression.

## Ups and downs

Don't expect to wake up one morning and find that things are getting better in a nice, straight line like a neat upwards graph. Postnatal depression plots a curious course. Some days seem like the beginning of the end and you will both see the sunshine and feel that you are finally getting there.

Don't sink into black depths of despair when the next day, things seem to be as bad as they ever were again. Postnatal depression is a roller coaster – it teases you with constant ups and downs. Eventually the bad days will become fewer and fewer and you'll notice after a while that all that's left are the good days again.

## Listen

The best gift you can give to a sufferer is that of listening. Even if you have heard the same things over and over, they make little sense or you don't agree – just listen. Don't judge, persuade, cajole or even offer an opinion – just nod, listen and be there.

## Give her time out

Offer the sufferer the chance to enjoy some space or time alone. Even if it's time for them to go shopping, sleep, have a quiet walk or a relaxing bath, this allows you quality time with the baby too. If possible, try to schedule in a regular 'slot'. This will give her something to look forward to and aim for throughout the rest of the week.

'Postnatal depression is a roller coaster – it teases you with constant ups and downs. Eventually the bad days will become fewer and fewer and you'll notice after a while that all that's left are the good days again.'

## Be there for her

Make sure you're there for her when needed. It can be frightening to be alone with the baby. This isn't because they are at any risk of hurting themselves or the baby, but because they find close personal contact too intense or overwhelming. Obviously this can be difficult to fit around work and other commitments and you may have to rearrange your usual routine for the duration of the illness, but again, keep remembering that the situation will get better – it's just a matter of time.

## Hands-on help

Offer as much practical help as possible – it's hard to be a carer and other commitments can be difficult to put off or rearrange. Try to set up a support network so that there is a whole safety net of help for the sufferer, friends and other family members should be called on during this time of need.

Think about some of the following and decide whether they are an option for you and your family: are there any household chores that could be delegated to paid help, e.g. cleaning or ironing? Is there someone who could listen out for the baby one afternoon per week so your loved one can sleep or rest? Can family and friends make extra casseroles for the freezer while they are cooking their own dinner? Instead of shopping at a supermarket, can you shop online instead?

# Taking care of the carers

This is a tough time for you too. Whether it's your wife, girlfriend, daughter or friend with postnatal depression, make no mistake it will be affecting you too. Make sure that you take steps to keep yourself happy and healthy too.

## Eat well

Eat three good, nutritious meals every day and drink plenty of fluid. This is the fuel that will allow you to care more effectively. Don't overlook your own needs.

## Rest well

Step back from your caring duties and your other roles in life. Take time to do nothing. Sit back, be aware of yourself and your feelings and breathe deeply and consciously.

## Stay well

Perhaps you have guided the sufferer towards medical help so don't be too proud to accept your own medicine. The experience of caring for someone with postnatal depression may be so intense that you might need to refer to health professionals too. If you don't want to see a GP, consider counselling.

Ensure there's someone in your life to listen to your feelings and concerns too. Dealing with someone else's emotional needs doesn't mean yours disappear. Make sure you deal with your issues and you will be able to take on board someone else's.

# Postnatal depression and dads

Recent studies have suggested that as many as 1 in 14 fathers may suffer with postnatal depression too (Mental Health Foundation, 2004).

The studies have identified almost identical symptoms to those found in their female counterparts. It's not a direct result of pregnancy and childbirth obviously. Men aren't subjected to the same biological, hormonal or psychological upsets that their female counterparts endure. There are various reasons why a father might suffer with a form of postnatal depression.

- If the woman in the relationship is experiencing postnatal depression, it becomes an exceptionally difficult time for a new father.

- Older fathers are more prone to depression – they find it harder to deal with the disruption to normal life routines and sleep patterns.

- First-time fathers are very vulnerable for the same reasons as older fathers. Their anxiety levels are also increased and they often experience intense pressure when they become the sole breadwinner of the family.

'This is a tough time for you too. Whether it's your wife, girlfriend, daughter or friend with postnatal depression, make no mistake it will be affecting you too.'

- Any man with a background history of depression will be particularly prone to depression following the birth of their baby.

- The dynamics of the relationship with their partner is suddenly changed and this can be very difficult to accept, triggering a depressive condition.

## Help for new fathers

The golden rule for new fathers is honesty, talking and more talking. If you feel depressed, confused or anxious, don't wait until you reach a crisis point – talk to your partner, friends, family or GP.

Men are under the misguided impression that they should get on with it and pull themselves together. The most responsible thing you can do, though, is to be honest about how you are feeling and seek help as soon as possible.

If it feels like this advice is too high a mountain to climb, try following this pathway towards your goal of better health.

- Start by accepting there are no short cuts or magic cures to postnatal depression. It's not something you can shake off, but it is something you can deal with. In the end, you will emerge from your experience better informed and emotionally rounder.

- Be honest with yourself, forget the idea that postnatal depression is 'a woman's thing'. Having a baby takes two people and the after-effects are felt by two people. It doesn't reflect on your masculinity and it is not your fault.

- Adopt the team strategy, even if it feels like no one else around you is. When women have babies, the entire healthcare system is geared up to supporting her through every stage with all the problems and concerns that come along too. Very little is ever addressed as far as dads are concerned. Remember, you are a team and your place in the team is every bit as important as that of mum. You aren't just 'the provider', the health and happiness of your family is only complete if you and the mother are both well. You have to leave the 'spare part' label behind and light a flashing neon sign over your head that pronounces to the world – 'vital part'.

- Don't wait to be asked, just tell people how you feel. The world often forgets fathers in this situation, so do yourself and your family a big favour and buck the trend – make your voice heard. Tell your wife, your friends and your family how you're feeling. This alone will release some of the pressure and make you feel better.

- Do some research and find some local support groups or clubs in your area. They may not be directly related to postnatal depression but will still offer you a talking outlet.

- You've come a long way down the road towards recovery but don't forget your GP. They are still your best hope of making a good steady recovery and offering you plenty of support and suggestions to make you and your family's life better.

# Summing Up

- Carers are often forgotten, but it's important to remember mothers are not the only victims of postnatal depression. There is plenty of help for the carers too, whether you are a father, grandmother or friend.

- Take steps to look after yourself and you will be an even better carer.

- Make sure you find out about postnatal depression, talk about it and be honest about your experiences.

- There are a few golden rules about caring for sufferers of postnatal depression. Look at this illness as a journey you are taking together, as with all journeys it will end and they will get better. Create space, time, comfort and security for the sufferer.

- New fathers are prone to depression too. Be aware and acquaint yourself with the steps you need to take to help yourself.

- Remember, good carers care for themselves.

# Chapter Ten

# Second Time Around

You would think that if you are already a mother, an extra baby will just fit in with you this time, but every baby is new and different. Being a mother is a fresh and unique experience no matter how many times you do it.

## Postnatal depression – all over again

The incidence of postnatal depression is much higher second time around. Various studies have estimated it may be up to 60%. However, nobody has ever pinned down why postnatal depression occurs once and we certainly can't say why you can get it twice.

It seems to be something you are 'prone' to. Patterns are evident in families and it stands to reason that if you have had postnatal depression once, you are more likely to get it a second time.

On the flip side, you may have sailed through your first experience of childbirth and motherhood, the second or third baby is born and the juggernaut of postnatal illness ploughs into you without any warning.

Just as every baby is different, every incidence of postnatal depression is different. So how do you cope with older children, a new baby and postnatal depression?

## Up against it

A baby takes up so much of your time and attention and having two children is doubly challenging. Any last remnants of 'me' time are finally sapped away.

'Every baby is new and different. Being a mother is a fresh and unique experience no matter how many times you do it.'

With your first baby, you are advised to rest when baby does, but of course, what happens when baby sleeps and your three-year-old wants to play? You play of course, and then the baby wakes up for a feed and it starts all over again. If you have passed a sleepless night with the baby, there is no chance to catch up with a well-deserved extra hour in bed to make up. Someone has to feed big brother or sister, pack them off to school or accompany them to playgroup. You are extra-tired and extra-short of time. These are some of the factors that can trigger postnatal depression.

A mother's relationship with her baby is the most intense love a human experiences. When there is the prospect of another baby to care for, mothers and fathers frequently wonder if they have a big enough heart to cope with two.

## Will I lose touch with my firstborn?

A common experience is the sense of loss mums encounter with the appearance of their subsequent children. They grieve for the time they lose with their older child or children. There's often a strong sense of guilt that you are displacing your other child or children and it's more intense if you throw postnatal depression into the mix.

## Shall I do it all over again?

People love to tell you that we 'forget' the dramas of childbirth, sleepless nights and all the physical discomforts. This is another myth, most mums remember all these things when the due date of their next child is looming. Second or third time around, we have past experiences and memories to deal with. Will the birth be easier? Will you cope? It all feeds our anxieties which can spiral out of proportion even before the new baby arrives. If you are predisposed to postnatal depression, it's a major cause of emotional stress.

Every new life is special in its own right but when you are already a mother, having another baby sometimes feels 'less special' if you are struggling with your emotions. There will be little time to rest and pamper yourself and you are often less kind to yourself than first-timers.

'With your first baby, you are advised to rest when baby does, but of course, what happens when baby sleeps and your three-year-old wants to play? You play of course, and then the baby wakes up for a feed and it starts all over again.'

You're a 'pro' aren't you? When you give birth for a second, third or fourth time, there is an increasing tendency for everyone to expect you to be back on your feet again within hours of giving birth. A new mum who has experienced a 'normal and routine birth' will normally leave hospital after fewer than 48 hours.

## Sibling troubles

New babies make a big impression on families and older siblings might feel moved away. If attention has suddenly been diverted to the new addition, it's no wonder their behaviour may become more challenging. They have to earn attention instead of receiving it as a birthright.

Even if this isn't the case and your other child is self-assured, welcoming and completely unaffected, your own guilt or concern for them threatens to overwhelm an over-burdened mother.

# So what can you do?

The key to tackling postnatal depression second time around is to attack it rather than react to it. It sounds like a big challenge but you can do it. Use faith and forethought as your two trusty tools.

## Knowing what to expect

You have lots of advantages on your side second time around. You know the warning signs, what to expect and you know when things don't 'feel' right. Everyone around you is better informed this time too.

## Stay positive

Don't spend your latest pregnancy dreading the worst, stay positive and tell yourself, lightning won't strike a second time. Be safe and secure with the thought that if it does, you have plans in place to help you deal with it.

'When you give birth for a second, third or fourth time, there is an increasing tendency for everyone to expect you to be back on your feet again with hours of giving birth.'

## Support yourself

Take extra care of yourself throughout your pregnancy and in the early days with the new baby. This includes taking plenty of rest (this isn't a luxury – it's an absolute must, a medicine). Eat a normal and healthy diet and make sure you get plenty of help with older children.

Set up a good support system during your pregnancy. If you have school-aged children, get someone to take a few school runs away from you, or ask friends or partners to accompany them to clubs and activities. You will be more rested and able to lavish special time and attention on your older child or children.

# Medical help

There's so much help a doctor can offer someone who is worried about experiencing postnatal depression again.

## Preventative antidepressants

Some doctors believe that there is a big argument for offering vulnerable mothers a course of antidepressants during the last few weeks of pregnancy. Some risks are attached to this and your doctor will want to discuss with you how these risks compare to leaving a developing condition untreated until after the birth. Also, the drugs can be selected to minimise any risks to the unborn child.

## Pregnancy counselling

A big crutch for the worried mother is psychological or talking support during their pregnancy, this is very effective. Therapies include straightforward counselling, sessions that deal with fears surrounding the birth, especially following a traumatic first birth or it may be something called cognitive behavioural therapy. This is a very effective method of learning to transform negative thought patterns into positive and productive ones.

## Hormone replacement therapy

Dr Katharina Dalton pioneered a controversial way to treat a recurrence of postnatal depression. Dr Dalton supported a hormonal approach to tackling the onset or return of postnatal depression.

Her plans included treating the mother with progesterone replacement therapies. The progesterone was intended to counter the massive drop in this hormone within minutes of the childbirth.

Some experts strongly believe that the natural fall-off of progesterone immediately after birth is often catastrophic for vulnerable new mothers. Other women have found that progesterone replacement contributes to their ill-health.

# Siblings

If you experience postnatal depression with a small baby and older children in tow, it's hard to imagine how you'll cope. Have faith in yourself, you will do it.

## Explain the changes

Make sure you constantly reassure older children that if they see Mummy upset or behaving differently (i.e. spending the whole day in pyjamas) it's only because she is trying to get used to having a new baby. This explains the changes in you and strikes a deep emotional chord with the child who is trying to do exactly the same thing.

## Ignore bad behaviour

Turn a 'blind' eye to some of your older child's behaviour. Things you would normally reprimand them for might be better ignored unless they are dangerous. If you draw attention to it, it sends signals to them that bad behaviour is a good way to grab your attention.

## Share rest times

Big brothers and sisters can get involved with rest times – when the baby is asleep, spend some relaxing time together. Pile up the cushions and fetch a stack of books to look through together. Have a cosy 'cinema' afternoon at home with popcorn, rugs and cuddles.

Spending this precious 'restful' time with your older child helps you focus and enjoy the simple pleasures of children without the nappies, crying and teething. Keep really physical activities for times when someone is able to take care of the baby and allow you some rest time afterwards.

'Spending this precious "restful" time with your older child helps you focus and enjoy the simple pleasures of children without the nappies, crying and teething.'

## Share responsibilities

Older siblings are always ready and willing to help with the baby. They love to fetch and carry – it gives them purpose and involvement and lightens your workload so don't be afraid to give small tasks to your other children.

# Summing Up

- Foresight is a great thing – the key to dealing with postnatal depression when you've experienced it before is to plan and prevent.

- Second time around, you are more susceptible to postnatal depression. This could be due to any number of physical, emotional or lifestyle factors. The point is nobody knows the exact cause, so consider attacking the condition on all fronts. If you 'expect' another bout and put all your plans in place, you will win either way. If you do get it, the effects will be lessened and dealt with far better and if you don't you will still benefit from your efforts.

- Your front line of attack should be the different ways in which you can put simple measures in place. Get plenty of rest and a good, healthy diet. As your due date approaches, put in place a strong and secure support network of friends and family. They can help you with chores, school runs and older children.

- The medical and health professions have lots of tools to help you too. Discuss the benefits of antidepressants during the final stages of your pregnancy if your GP thinks that's appropriate. Think about hormone replacement or talking therapies.

- Find ways to involve any older children with your experiences, make sure they stay happy and healthy with lots of cuddles, kind words and love.

- In the same way you make a birth plan, make a wellbeing plan for yourself and consider all these ideas to give yourself a fighting chance of dealing with postnatal depression differently this time around.

# Chapter Eleven

# Treatments: Antidepressants

'I don't want to go on tablets,' is an understandable response to the possibility of medication. There's a flood of myths which do nothing for the cause of antidepressants. Tie this up with all the horror stories in the media or old-fashioned prejudice and ignorance and it's no wonder that antidepressants are often seen as non-starters or absolutely the last resort.

However, if you were suffering from an ongoing illness like kidney disease, asthma or diabetes, there wouldn't be many objections to medications offered to make a recovery or relieve symptoms for these illnesses. There is still a feeling that taking antidepressants is a sign of weakness and failure and you'll succumb to the mind-altering drugs, never to be the same again.

With understanding, thought and choice, antidepressants can be a good prop if you feel smothered by postnatal depression.

'With understanding, thought and choice, antidepressants can be a good prop if you feel smothered by postnatal depression.'

## Why choose antidepressants?

Choosing antidepressants could be seen as a sign of strength – you are doing something about the way you feel which will improve life for you, your baby and your family immeasurably.

Nobody need 'succumb'. With a little knowledge about how the drugs work, taking antidepressants is an informed and intelligent choice.

Antidepressants alter brain chemicals not your mind. You won't be feeling different but you will feel better.

# Types of antidepressants

There are many personality types, all driven by the brain and its chemical make-up. Antidepressants act on the chemicals of the brain, so to ensure that they reflect the different chemical make-up, a whole range of antidepressant types have been developed since their first appearance in the 1950s.

A drug which suits 'Patient A' may be totally unsuitable for 'Patient B'. Patient B's GP will need to reconsider which type of antidepressant is better and will make a revised choice based on the side effects experienced and the type of depression Patient B is experiencing.

The drugs address the chemical imbalances within the brain that are thought to contribute to the patient's condition. This is done by affecting the levels of neurotransmitters in the brain. Neurotransmitters are chemicals that conduct electrical impulses to the nerves or neurons of the brain cells.

Bear in mind that all drugs have potential side effects and the manufacturers have a duty to outline any possibility. Everyone is different and you may experience no side effects at all or you may experience some mildly or severely – ensure you review any medication with your GP if you do experience any side effects that cause you problems.

## Tricyclics

Tricyclics are the oldest generation of antidepressants. They work on a similar principle to their younger counterparts, however, they are less targeted at specific brain chemicals and tend to cause greater side effects as a result. Tricyclics sometimes make users feel drowsy or sedated and this is a non-starter if you have a young baby. Medical professionals are less likely to prescribe these as a first resort.

## SSRI antidepressants

SSRIs were the new wonder drugs that knocked the tricyclics off their perch. They specifically react on the brain chemical serotonin (the 'feel-good' hormone), by preventing it from being broken down. This raises serotonin levels within the brain. It was found to increase mood and lessen depressive feelings.

They have fewer side effects than tricyclics because they are more specific. The side effects can include insomnia, anxiety and reduced sexual function.

SSRIs can take between two and four weeks to work and as time passes, they continue to raise your mood. Even at four weeks, it's too early to appreciate their full effect. This shows how important it is to be patient and let the drugs work as they should.

## SNRI antidepressants

SNRIs were developed as another step forward from SSRIs. Working on the same principle as SSRIs, they also affect the brain chemical noradrenalin. They are often prescribed if SSRIs are not successful.

## MAOI antidepressants

Drugs falling into this category are rarely prescribed. The chemical make-up of the drug can cause serious reactions with other drugs or substances. These even include everyday food items.

Anyone prescribed one of these drugs needs careful supervision and a controlled diet. MAOIs work differently by affecting enzymes that interact with the brain chemicals rather than the chemicals themselves.

# Taking antidepressants if you are pregnant or breastfeeding

You can't get away from the fact that antidepressants will reach your baby if taken during pregnancy or breastfeeding.

Some antidepressants are off the agenda if they have implications for the baby's health, but there are plenty of alternatives. These will only reach your baby in very small amounts and are easily discharged by the baby's body.

Plenty of women choose to breastfeed even if they are taking in higher levels of antidepressant, long-term effects on babies are relatively unknown, but there have been no serious concerns or evidence to cause alarm.

You need to balance the pros with the cons. If you leave depression untreated, would it have far worse consequences for your family's future health and wellbeing? Think about other forms of treatment that could be used alongside reduced levels of medication or in place of antidepressants.

Don't disregard traditional medication because of pregnancy or breastfeeding. Make informed choices and educate yourself about the options. Your GP and health visitor will always be keen to support your decisions.

'Think about other forms of treatment that could be used alongside reduced levels of medication or in place of antidepressants.'

# Stopping antidepressants

When antidepressants start to work, don't make the mistake of thinking all is well so you can stop the tablets and 'go back to normal'. Most GPs recommend a period of at least six months with the medication. This gives time for recovery and helps to prevent any future recurrence.

Before you take any steps to withdraw, it's essential that you do so under the guidance of your GP. Stopping suddenly can be very dangerous.

Antidepressants are not addictive but they may cause some withdrawal symptoms when you stop. To make the process easier, most health professionals recommend you taper off or gradually reduce your treatment instead.

## Follow your GP's advice

Arm yourself with knowledge about any possible side effects. This makes the process feel more controlled – don't over-research and 'talk' yourself into experiencing a long list of symptoms though.

Make sure you have the support of your partner, friends or family. They need to know what you are doing.

Choose a time to withdraw when life feels settled and secure. Don't pick the run-up to Christmas or just before a holiday, for example.

# Dos and don'ts

Follow all the guidelines and advice you are given and your experience of antidepressants should be a positive one.

## Do

- Find out as much as possible about antidepressants and the different ways they work. Explore and discuss all of your options with your GP.

- Take your medicine at the same time every day, get into a routine and make it a part of your daily life. Some medications require one tablet per day while others require two, one in the morning and another at night.

- Keep your tablets somewhere safe, they are very harmful to anyone other than you in the correct doses. This is vital in a household where there are children present.

- Think about combining your medication with other treatments such as cognitive behavioural therapy, counselling or relaxation treatments. Depression is usually more complex than a straightforward chemical imbalance. The jury is still out on the exact causes, so attack the situation on all fronts.

- Allow plenty of time for the tablets to work. Many antidepressants need two to four weeks to reach their full effect. When you feel well, you should allow at least six months on the medication.

- Visit your GP regularly for check-ups and reviews. This includes talking about how you feel and vital medical tests like blood pressure.

- Seek advice if you experience any side effects when you start taking the tablets. Your GP may alter your dose, change the medication to another or if the effects are mild, advise you to wait a little longer until your general mood improves.

- Check to see if you need to avoid any other substances. St John's wort and alcohol can both have dramatic effects when they interact with antidepressants.

## Don't

- Assume you can take other substances because they are 'herbal' or 'natural'. They can still affect your medication.

- Alter your dose depending on how you feel. You need to keep even, level and regular doses. It's never advisable to change the details of your prescription without consulting your GP or health practitioner.

- Think that antidepressants will completely cure your depression. They relieve the symptoms but you have to search for an underlying cause in your life too.

- Be discouraged if a particular type of antidepressant isn't for you. One size does not fit all. Every brain is different and there will be a medication to suit yours.

# Summing Up

■ Don't discount antidepressants. They have been developed over the years to a stage where there will be something to suit everyone.

■ Do plenty of research. Work with your GP to find the best medication for you and consider complementary routes to recovery, like counselling.

■ Don't make any assumptions about antidepressants or listen to any myths. There are plenty of misconceptions out there and to miss out on valuable treatment as a result would be a sad and misguided mistake.

# Chapter Twelve

# Treatments: Alternative Ideas

There are an astounding number of options available for the treatment of postnatal depression. Not all of them are considered 'traditional' and some are positively controversial but they are all worth considering.

## Words of warning

A lot of people believe you are better off with alternative remedies because they are 'natural'. Many traditional medicines and drugs are made from natural substances but they are only available by prescription as they can cause an overdose or bad reaction if taken incorrectly. Just because something is 'herbal' or 'natural', it doesn't mean that you can take it freely without medical advice and equally, just because something is only available on prescription it doesn't mean it's unnatural.

Even if you choose to go down a different route with your treatment plan, involve your GP or a health professional first.

'Just because something is "herbal" or "natural", it doesn't mean that you can take it freely without medical advice.'

## St John's wort

The benefits of St John's wort as a herbal alternative to traditional antidepressants have been trumpeted for years. The substance is a perfect reminder to treat natural remedies with great care. Some of the most toxic poisons and medications known to humankind are derived from plants, such as the use of foxglove (digitalis) in heart medicines.

St John's wort is no exception, some people report its effects on mild to moderate depression are very impressive and others have experienced side effects similar to prescribed antidepressants.

St John's wort (hypericum) is a plant bearing small yellow flowers and has been used to treat conditions for hundreds of years. It's easily found in health-food shops and supermarkets, usually in the form of tablets or capsules.

There is no solid proof that the drug works. It's thought that St John's wort has an effect on the chemicals in the brain such as serotonin and noradrenalin. It seems to alter the balance of these neurotransmitters in a way that's similar to SSRI antidepressants.

The similarity doesn't end there. You should allow two to four weeks for the full effect of the plant to become evident. It also has a growing effect on the mood.

The major advantage of St John's wort is that the side effects are less obvious and milder than traditional antidepressants.

Bear in mind that it's powerful enough to have a negative effect on any antidepressants that are taken in addition, as well as blood-thinning medications and the contraceptive pill. All drugs and therapies traditionally recommended by doctors are tested rigorously before they are licensed for public use. Very little research and testing has been carried out on alternative remedies and therapies, such as St John's wort. It must be taken only after professional advice, and avoided if you are breastfeeding or pregnant.

## Hormone replacement therapy

The clues are all there. Following childbirth, the levels of progesterone drop by 120% and there are massive changes in the levels of oestrogen too. Think about the profound effect this hormonal cocktail has on a woman's physical and mental health throughout her life, such as during menstrual cycle, pregnancy, childbirth and the menopause. Medical research often points to hormonal treatments as a possible route to follow when treating postnatal depression.

# What's the treatment?

Dr Dalton's ideas were to treat the new mother immediately after the birth with a mixture of pessaries and injections in the hope that by rebalancing the hormones, the effects of postnatal depression would be chased away. For some mothers this makes perfect sense as progesterone is a natural substance which poses little risk to her or her baby if she is breastfeeding.

It is still a controversial approach and some doctors discount it as a treatment, so you may need to do a bit of research during your pregnancy. A few interesting websites that provide useful background information based on Dr Katharina Dalton's ideas about hormone therapy are:

- www.progesteronelink.com – this website contains fascinating information about progesterone therapy.

- www.natural-progesterone-advisory-network.com – a comprehensive insight into the issue of hormone replacement. It carries a lot of references to Dr Dalton's life and research.

- www.naprotechnology.com – this website features a good page dedicated to postnatal depression and Dr Dalton.

Please bear in mind these tend to be commercially-based websites, there's actually very little non-commercial advice available, but I have tried to choose websites that have an information-bias.

# Nutritional therapy

A good, balanced diet is an important part of recovering from postnatal depression. Research has looked at diet to provide specific answers about treating postnatal depression more effectively.

Some of the ideas lie with the nutrients that are literally drained from the mother during her pregnancy. Experts suggest that deficiencies of these substances could contribute significantly to postnatal depression. Popular theories suggest new mothers should increase their levels of zinc, vitamin B, magnesium and omega-3 fatty acids.

'Experts suggest that deficiencies of these substances could contribute significantly to postnatal depression. Popular theories suggest new mothers should increase their levels of zinc, vitamin B, magnesium and omega-3 fatty acids.'

No two bodies are the same, nutritional deficiencies and the body's reactions to these are bound to differ. It makes sense to try all the different options and see if they work for you. Consider making an appointment to visit a dietitian that specialises in postnatal care.

# Complementary therapies

These approaches to recovery are useful to complement other approaches, rather than as stand alone treatments. It seems that one therapy can work well for some mothers and not for others.

Complementary therapies deal with postnatal depression on a wider front. Instead of treating a narrow range of problems with medication, this branch of medicine takes a much wider approach that aims to help the whole body, the emotions and the spirits to recover. Complementary therapies are a chance for you to experiment and find something that appeals to you.

- Acupuncture is an ancient Chinese practice using metallic needles inserted at specific points across the skin. This is said to relieve and reopen the energy pathways.

- Aromatherapy uses essential oils, often combined with massage, to have profound effects on the emotions and heighten wellbeing or create feelings of relaxation or rejuvenation.

- Hypnotherapy aims to tap into the deeper levels of the mind to promote healing and positive thought patterns.

- Light therapy first became popular in the treatment of SAD (seasonal affective disorder) and uses concentrated light rays to rebalance hormones and create a sense of wellbeing.

- Homeopathy uses minute levels of natural plant extracts to trigger the natural healing abilities of the human body and mind.

- Reflexology works on the principle that medical conditions can be treated by manipulating the soles of the feet. They are thought to contain all the relevant nerve endings from the body.

- Osteopathy treats joints and muscles throughout the body in order to benefit other health conditions.

If a method works for you, do the mechanics of the treatment really matter? The results and the way you feel afterwards are the most important things to consider and by using conventional medical treatments alongside complementary therapies you may find the path to recovery is eased. As emphasised before, not everything works for everyone – bear in mind that we're all individuals and you are free to decide what is best for your circumstances.

For more information see, *Complementary Therapies – The Essential Guide* (Need2Know).

## Intensive relaxation techniques

Sometimes it's tough to slow your thoughts down. Some sufferers are unable to sleep and others report a sense of being hyperactive or manic. It makes sense to think about ways to relax mind and body, particularly at a time when there is so little opportunity to be selfish.

Relaxation is something you should try to build into your life every day – at best this is tough and at worst, it's impossible. Maybe the answer lies in making relaxation part of your structured recovery plan. It helps to reduce blood pressure and breathing rates, while increasing the feeling of wellbeing and decreasing stress and anxiety.

Therapies to try include: massage, yoga, Pilates, meditation and deep breathing exercises. To learn the techniques properly, make an appointment with a practitioner in one of the areas that interests you. This also ensures you have made a commitment to take time out for yourself.

'It makes sense to think about ways to relax mind and body, particularly at a time when there is so little opportunity to be selfish.'

# Summing Up

- Everyone's experience of postnatal depression is different and they must treat their condition in a way that suits them.

- You could try less conventional methods than those your GP may be able to offer. A lot of these alternative treatments are still a mystery to science. The important thing is if they make you feel better, that's all you need to know.

- Consult your GP and make sure that it's safe to undertake these treatments in conjunction with their advice and any medication you're taking.

- Don't ever assume because things are natural that they are without risks or safety issues. Remember that the most powerful substances known to humankind are 'natural'. All treatments must be treated with care and respect.

Need2Know

# Chapter Thirteen

# Treatments:
# Talking it Over

If there is one thing you can do to make things better, it's talking. Talking to your friends, family and GP sets the ball rolling. Don't underestimate the power of talking as a proper and powerful treatment. Use the talking therapies by themselves and alongside treatments prescribed by your GP or alternative therapies.

## Talking to friends and family

'A problem shared is a problem halved', became a proverb because it's a powerful truth. No emotional burdens seem quite so mountainous when they're shared around the fire, kitchen table or bar. By sharing issues and concerns, powerful changes start to take place between you and your listener. You create a bond and pact of trust which strengthens a valuable human relationship.

By involving another person in the workings of your mind and your emotional turmoil, you are inviting new thoughts and ideas from the outside world. Perhaps your listener has had a similar experience which will help you to plan a way through the journey.

Talking shatters the 'stigma' of your emotional difficulties. The moment people start to talk and be open about their experiences, taboos disappear and you gain respect and admiration for your ability to share. It's a mark of strength.

'By sharing issues and concerns, powerful changes start to take place between you and your listener. You create a bond and pact of trust which helps strengthen a valuable human relationship.'

# Counselling

Counselling is the simplest and purest of formal talking therapies. It's one step up from the talking therapy you might have set in motion with your family and friends.

Counselling is all about you, and your therapist will make sure that your sessions together make you feel safe.

For counselling to work, you need to know that everything you say will be treated in confidence, with respect and without being judged. The therapist listens without the 'closeness' that could get in the way when you talk to friends and family. This makes you feel more able to discuss experiences, thoughts or feelings about your life.

If you can't see any way through the fogginess of your depression, a counsellor will be able to hold a torch for you. They won't tell you which path or route to follow but they will make sure that they give you enough light to help you find your own way.

# Cognitive behavioural therapy

Cognitive behavioural therapy illustrates the idea that humans are full of prejudices and habits which colour the way they think about the world around them. We are programmed to look at something, or experience something and react, according to the presets we have stored in our heads.

Cognitive behavioural therapy aims to stop this process by taking apart the way you think and rebuilding your thoughts in a way which is more appropriate, positive and helpful. Your reactions to life and its varied tapestry of events are calmer and better thought through. It forms a really strong bond between thinking and behaviour.

Cognitive behavioural therapy is a powerful talking therapy, you will need to commit months to the programme but your therapist will give you skills that last a lifetime.

# Psychotherapy

Psychotherapy has fascinated people for years. It started with the belief that we are all driven by a part of our mind that is unconscious, almost instinctive. Daily life and its constant challenges make us react in ways we can't possibly understand until we tap in to and analyse this unconscious part of our thinking.

Psychotherapists believe we get all these thought patterns from things that have happened to us in the past or from our childhoods. Everything about us forms a set of beliefs and patterns that lie deeply buried until uncovered by the psychotherapist.

# Life coaching

Life coaching is a relatively new form of talking therapy, its popularity has grown in recent years to reflect the effective way it helps people to change their lives forever.

A combination of counselling and cognitive behavioural therapy, life coaching attempts to uncover the reasons why you conduct your life in the ways you do. When these have been exposed, the life coach will help you to adjust your personal outlook and thought patterns.

This will give the individual a set of practical solutions to make their lives better with a more positive outlook. It empowers you to an extent where you can set yourself achievable goals and it creates a positive atmosphere for you to lay down future plans.

# Neuro-linguistic programming

It sounds like a grand name but it's a surprisingly simple idea. Neuro-linguistic programming is quite a new science and starts with the idea that to make life a more positive experience, we need to understand how the brain works.

'A combination of counselling and cognitive behavioural therapy, life coaching attempts to uncover the reasons why you conduct your life in the ways you do.'

Neuro-linguistic programming works out thought patterns that the individual uses to react to situations and why people act the way they do. Neuro-linguistic programming therapists help you to discover the maps and patterns of your thought processes that stop you from achieving goals in your life.

Taking these patterns as a template, they are then able to recommend a series of exercises and activities that turn all these preset brain programmes upside down.

## Group therapy

'A group is support at its very best. Numbers mean strength and you can all share lots of different views, ideas and options.'

Talking about the way you feel to a group of people rather than a single person feels like a huge cliff to scale. It's an incredibly strong form of talking therapy and you'd be wise to think seriously about taking part in a regular group meeting.

To get exactly what you need from it you have to be careful to pick the right group. Ask health professionals if they can recommend a group or do some research yourself – try your local library, the Internet or perhaps friends and family have some suggestions.

Group therapy is headed by a trained therapist, someone who guides and advises the group in a gentle and subtle way. The members of the group are the real workers in this situation and the whole experience is intensely useful with so many benefits.

### Why choose group therapy?

You're not alone. With a group you feel part of something special when postnatal depression has made you feel unusual, excluded or isolated. It's hugely reassuring and a relief to realise the way you feel and think is perfectly normal and shared or recognised by the others in the group.

A group is support at its very best. Numbers mean strength and you can all share lots of different views, ideas and options. Some therapists use group relaxation techniques, so the group feel like they are taking part in shared learning together.

Rose ran a hugely successful support group for several years and feels their role in recovery from postnatal depression is unrivalled:

'The sharing of information and help in a group situation is always very useful and a good way to raise self-esteem. I found that my support groups moved on a lot quicker than a lot of other groups and my clients seemed to fare better. I started to ask myself why.

'I soon realised that the reason was I was "coaching" them, giving life skills and encouraging their natural skills and ambitions. They were able to share what they were feeling and fully express themselves. If there were any anger issues or other negative emotions, they were able to air this within the group rather than going for their partner's jugular the minute he walked through the door. The group was a place where they could build long-lasting relationships and new life skills.

'I always told my clients not to regret having postnatal depression because they would learn so much at the end of it. They were able to cope with things they never thought they could cope with before. They would discover talents that they never knew they had.

'First of all, you must "acknowledge" the postnatal depression because you can't change what you don't acknowledge. Many live in denial or have a "victim" mentality. They blame different circumstances or people for how they are feeling.

'Get the social support you need and get the medical support you need. If it's possible, join a support group. Don't be secretive and think that it's just your problem and yours to sort out. It's a family problem, if you have family and friends who want to help, all the better.'

# Summing Up

- Talking is the most powerful way to change things. It helps you build bridges and find your way through to the other side.

- You can use talking therapies in conjunction with other treatments like prescribed medicine or alternative therapies. However, talking is such a strong tool that some new mothers find that it's enough for them on its own.

- The simplest form of therapy is talking to friends and family. However, some people feel safer and more able to open their lives and be perfectly honest with a third party without emotional attachment.

- The first level of talking therapies is counselling which takes a step away from friends and family, but works in a similar way. Some people find their way into group therapy which is an excellent way to make you feel normal and supported.

- There are lots of other forms of talking therapies, such as cognitive behavioural therapy, neuro-linguistic programming and psychotherapy. Each works in a slightly different way but with the same results and following the same route – talking, talking and more talking.

# Chapter Fourteen

## People Like You

It's an instant tonic to discover that you are following pathways that people have discovered long before you. Just by uncovering other people's stories, you get an insight into postnatal depression. You encounter all its differing effects, the ways to cope and reassurance that life will be bright and happy as it was before.

Take some time to read through these stories of people who have lived through postnatal depression. They are real people and real events. Every story is different but the outcome is always the same. They got better, just like you will.

## Maria's story

Maria suffered with postnatal depression after her first child was born. She believes that as a newcomer to the UK, the loneliness she suffered contributed to a condition which caused her to be sectioned.

'With the birth of my first child I suffered severe postnatal depression, a condition that I was never aware of at the time. During my pregnancy, I carried on as before and believed I could do so after the birth of the baby. Nothing prepared me for the complete changes ahead, literally everything changed.

'Within weeks of the birth (an emergency caesarean), I became a different person, almost detached from my real self. I tried so hard to fight the changes that I was experiencing, to this day the thoughts I had at that time are still blurred. It is as if it wasn't me.

'There were several episodes of abnormal behaviour that I was having at the time, like cold sweats when the baby cried and crying with him, helpless. I panicked over the smallest, most insignificant things, with an overwhelming sense of being useless and incapable. Being a mother was supposed to be a magical and enjoyable experience, I was ashamed and in denial that I had none of those feelings. I felt useless, trapped, unhappy and guilty.

'I didn't want to disappoint anyone. The people that knew me thought of me as always being on top of everything. I made it all seem effortless and I gave a very secure positive image to everyone. I remember thinking that it was like being in a play, I used to think on my way to work, "Showtime, look happy, and don't forget the smile". It made me feel like a fake but I had to do it, anything else was admitting to terrible failure on my part.

'I felt that there was nothing good in my life and the baby was an affirmation of how useless I had become. I hated the feeling of having no control over anything. Slowly the possibility of ending my life became a relief. Planning it and thinking about it made me feel in control of something. It answered all my worries. I couldn't think of anything better, it would give me an escape from that awful, lonely and unhappy place that I was at.

'I needed someone to talk to, to tell me that I was normal, to be cared for, consoled and listened to. I wanted to talk openly about my thoughts and feelings without being scared of what they would think of me.

'Things were very different for me, mothers should never be made to feel ashamed, failed or labelled as "mad". I was eventually sectioned and not once did anyone think to diagnose or consider postnatal depression. I was put in a room and never left on my own, not even to go to the toilet. I was a danger to my own baby, how low could you go?

'Education about this issue is essential, it could happen to anyone. I was born and grew up in another country and I had no family or close friends at the time, this played a huge part in the dramatic way my health deteriorated.

'Unfortunately, I was never aware that I could talk to my GP or health visitor about it.

'I feel very optimistic about the way things are changing. Postnatal depression isn't taboo anymore, it's talked about a lot and many high-profile celebrities have been very open about their experiences. I do get cross when some public figures use it to raise their public profile though. It angers me when they present the condition in a "sexed-up" way with a distorted picture that detracts from the reality of genuine cases.

'Understanding and knowledge of postnatal depression is very important. I used it to gain the strength to help myself, through reading about others that have been through the same or similar experiences. That's how I started on the road to recovery.'

# Carrie's story

Carrie experienced postnatal depression after her second child was born. Luckily, she was supported by a strong family unit and an understanding GP.

'I was really looking forward to having a sibling for my first child, our family would feel complete. I had suffered with post-traumatic stress with my first delivery and received cognitive behavioural therapy, so I was very aware of the things that could happen.

'I first became aware that things were not as they should be when I developed an overwhelming feeling of negativity a few months after the baby was born. I hated the way I looked. I seemed to have no patience particularly with my elder daughter and husband. It then turned into a total feeling of failure and deep unhappiness.

'My relationship with my husband became very strained as I didn't tell him any of the feelings that I was experiencing. I just felt angry all the time and as I was exhausted due to sleep deprivation, I thought it was because of that. I ate constantly! I piled on the weight and hated the way I looked. I fluctuated from utter rage to crying uncontrollably. I felt completely out of control inside but kept up an appearance on the outside.

'My GP was fantastic. He made me feel comfortable and at ease. I always felt that I was making a bigger deal of my symptoms but he always reassured me that they were real and they could be dealt with.

'One of the areas that caused a lot of stress for me was looking after the kids and doing all the housework. I had to learn to relax my expectations so I wasn't setting myself up for failure. My husband was brilliantly supportive. At weekends, he would let me have some "me" time and always encouraged me to do something. My sister and mother visited a lot, so they were pretty supportive.

'I had cognitive behavioural therapy and counselling to stop negative thinking. I found it very useful and still do. I am acutely aware if I start with any unhelpful thinking.

'I have very high, sometimes too high, expectations of myself and criticise my mothering skills often. I have learnt to relax about things that are beyond my control and have come to really enjoy my time with both of my children.'

## Alice's story

Following a traumatic caesarean section, Alice suffered postnatal depression but made a good recovery and went on to have a second child without a recurrence of the condition.

'I didn't have a clue what to expect from being a mother. I had attended the NCT classes which focused purely on the birth. I read every baby and pregnancy magazine going which had successfully "glamourised" pregnancy, birth and raising a child. I felt that having a baby was the most natural thing in the world!

'We had been trying for a baby for a year and a half before falling pregnant; sadly, I had a miscarriage at six weeks. I was devastated. Fortunately, I fell pregnant with Emma two months later. However, I had a difficult pregnancy with frequent bleeding and the fear of losing the baby again constantly terrified me.

'After a C-section birth, I heard Emma cry and felt immediate relief that my baby was safe. Emma was then checked over by the hospital staff and was handed to my husband. I was the last one in the room to hold my baby, which broke my heart. I was her mother who had carried her for nine months and now having gone through a very traumatic birth, I felt like the least important person in the room and to this day it still causes great pain when I think about it.

'After the C-section, I felt like I had physically been cut in two. I couldn't believe that after such a major operation I was expected to get up the following day. I was experiencing excruciating pain and the midwives were far too busy to help me much with the baby.

'At home Emma didn't sleep well but even when she did, I didn't rest; I mowed the lawn, tidied the house and did the washing. At night, it took me hours to return back to sleep after getting up to feed Emma. I felt numb and overwhelmed by the responsibility of looking after a baby, guilty that I was doing everything wrong. I felt that I was living in a very dark place. In terms of caring for Emma, I felt emotionally detached, there were times that I didn't even feel like her real mother and that I was borrowing her for a while. I was determined to look after her until her real mother came back for her, so I meticulously took care of her needs almost as if I was going to be judged at the end of my time with her.

'On visiting the doctor, I was prescribed antidepressants and within days of taking them, I started to feel better. I took these for six months and then decided to wean myself off them. I then took daily doses of St John's wort. A few months later, I started to suffer with panic attacks. I went to see another doctor who referred me for counselling. I had approximately three months of treatment which I found to be life-changing. My therapist was superb, never judging, never blaming and he really helped me to explore why I might have felt the way I did about events.

'About seven weeks after having Emma, I started to attend a local baby group and met up with a fellow new mum. She started to talk about her experience with postnatal depression after having her first child. This lady helped me a great deal in the following months and again when I was expecting my second child.

'My coping strategies for living with postnatal depression were to develop a routine for the day-to-day struggles of having a baby. The treatment I received gave me the confidence to try to implement a routine, Emma certainly seemed more settled from there on in. I started taking time out by myself whether that be taking a walk or going for a massage.

'Two years later, I fell pregnant with my second child. My expectations of having a child were much more realistic this time round, however, I felt that I needed support while pregnant to help me through. I contacted my therapist who had started to specifically treat pregnant ladies who suffered previous traumatic birth experiences. I had a course of hypnotherapy sessions which really helped. I also turned to a good friend for support who suffered with postnatal depression and a traumatic birth and had gone on to have a second child.

'At times after the birth of my second baby, I felt overwhelmed with the responsibility of caring for two small children and couldn't believe that I was back in the world of sleepless nights. During this time, I continually questioned myself when I had a "down" day, whether this was the start of things to come. My friend reminded me that you instinctively know when you are suffering from postnatal depression and the fact that I was questioning myself would suggest that I wasn't.

'My one piece of advice would be never to decline any "genuine" offers of help! Whether it is someone to help with the baby for a while, cook for you or listen when you need to talk.'

## Bella's story

Bella expected to be a good mum and was terrified when the reality didn't match up to her expectations.

'I expected to be a natural mum as I had always spent a lot of time around children. I wanted to be perfect.

'We completed our plans to buy a new house when Jay was just a week or so old, so we had a house move to contend with as well as a newborn. The day we moved into the house, I realised I felt lost. I sat on the doorstep and thought, what have I done? I remember crying and again felt I had lost control of everything. I convinced myself that social services would come to my door and try to take the baby away from me.

'My partner Lewis was then offered a new job with shift work, so he was out early or back late. I found it very difficult to be alone during this time so I spent my life at my mum's house. To me we had a house but not a home and I felt very unsettled. I felt like I didn't belong anywhere and I just wanted to feel normal.

'I remember some people saying to me that I should pull myself together and I was lucky the baby slept and didn't scream. This just made me feel like a more useless human being than I already did.

'I found day-to-day life so hard and needed a lot of sleep as I didn't have any energy. I didn't care what I looked like and I smoked more and more.

96

'To make myself feel better, I made small changes to my daily life. I made sure that as soon as I was up, I was washed and dressed. I felt worse lounging in my pyjamas all day and this made me less likely to go straight back to bed as soon as Lewis walked in the door. I tried to take Jay for a walk every day, even if I was at my mum's house. The fresh air gave me a clearer head. Also, I made greetings cards and read lots of books and magazines. I used to love reading to Jay even at a very young age. He was able to read very early on in his life and I believe this is due to me reading to him when I felt so bad.

'After seeing a GP, I was put on antidepressants and it took me a long time to accept that I needed these to help me. I used to look at other mothers and think, "Do you need a pill to get you through the day? No, probably not, then why do I?" The pills were kept hidden from Lewis as I felt he was constantly checking on me. I learned the hard way that there was nothing to be ashamed of and I gradually accepted that I needed them, so if I was going to get better, I would have to take them.

'My health visitor was brilliant and I still don't know to this day how I would have got through without her and the postnatal depression support group I went to.

'Postnatal depression affected me for a good three and a half years, on and off. Had I accepted the truth and the pills much sooner, then maybe I wouldn't have suffered that long. The illness has made me a stronger, more confident person and I no longer look back to the past and think "what if?" The most important thing that I learnt was that life isn't always easy but with courage and determination, I can get through anything. The worst thing ever is to be told to "pull yourself together".'

## Audrey's story

Audrey offers the valuable perspective of a mother helplessly watching her own daughter struggle with motherhood and postnatal depression.

'My daughter Jane suffered with postnatal depression. I had no previous experience of the illness. I was part of a large circle of mothers about my age in the 1970s, they were all stay-at-home mothers and as far as I know not one of them suffered with postnatal depression. It was not even talked about. About two weeks after my son was born I felt a bit down but was told to get up and get on with it as I had no choice.

'The first thing I noticed was within days of my granddaughter's birth, Jane seemed too "bright" and it felt like she was putting on an act. I almost believed her.

'About six months after the birth, my husband and I noticed a big change in Jane. She seemed moody, weepy, unreasonable and confrontational. Jane resented other people's freedom, as if she was mourning a way of life.

'As grandparents and parents we felt totally useless, sad, worried and frustrated. We were fearful for our son-in-law who was virtually on his own coping with the illness, a new baby and a full-time job. We were very worried and tried to be positive by listening and helping with advice or babysitting. Thankfully, after our second grandchild was born Jane was clued-up enough to recognise the symptoms and get it treated before it took a hold.

'My advice would be to be very, very open and alert to the fact that it could happen to your daughter even if she was usually in control of her life before the baby arrived.'

## Justine's story

Justine's world fell apart when she felt she wasn't able to be as good a mother to her second child as she was to her first.

'I felt my second pregnancy was contaminated by the marriage break-up of close members of our family for shocking reasons. I also desperately wanted to move house.

'Having my daughter was a very positive experience; I felt that I'd been a really good mum. I expected to love it as much second time around. Poor old Sam was just a "normal" baby but my daughter had been so exceptionally contented, his crying was a nasty shock. He had an incessant hunger, which I felt I couldn't meet and I didn't want to bottle-feed. I think my blissful relationship with my first child led me to have unrealistic expectations of myself.

'Suddenly, it all felt scary. I didn't trust myself anymore to be able to supply the needs of my children. I felt like a bad mother all the time. I went on to antidepressants when the baby was 14 weeks old. They helped me for a while but then I really lost the plot. I became so profoundly depressed and convinced the children were irretrievably harmed by me that life became intolerable.

'Looking back, I think having a baby is such a responsibility I would encourage every woman to take time to reflect and prepare for that. I've learnt loads about myself and I think I've grown in compassion and the ability to listen because of it. I have also learnt that children, especially in a stable, loving relationship are very resilient.

'It's a wonderful thing to be well again and to be a mum. Very little is black or white. The present is a gift and awful times do pass. My husband used to say, "This feels all-consuming but it will be an increasingly small chapter in our children's lives". I think that's true as I've learnt that "this too will pass".'

## John's story

John has witnessed postnatal depression through the eyes of a husband, a father and a clinical psychologist – a unique viewpoint.

'Justine's depression had a gradual onset after our second child was born. It became increasingly severe and eventually required hospitalisation seven months after our son was born.

'By nature, Justine is someone with strong opinions and sets herself high standards. She was self-critical when these were not reached. As a clinical psychologist, as well as her husband, I wonder whether this was an illness waiting to happen when sufficient stressors combined to trigger an underlying vulnerability.

'For me, the experience of being the husband to a wife with severe depression was huge and highly complex. I was a committed husband, determined not to lose a wonderful wife and the mother of our children. I was a committed father, determined to nurture our children and protect them from the suffering or harm that an emotionally (and sometimes physically) absent mother might bring.

'My other role was as a professional clinical psychologist, determined to bring to bear all my professional knowledge and skills to understand the situation, help others understand and to access the best treatment and care. I found lots of strength from a wonderfully caring set of family and friends, as well as from an honest and open relationship with God.

'One of the most difficult aspects of Justine's depression was her tendency towards suicide. At points of real crisis, I had to remain as emotionally detached as possible so I could make wise judgements and share the situation with people around me. The personal impact of living with the real possibility of losing Justine was horrifying.

'Recovery from depression was not just the process of Justine's mental health improving. We had to work together to adjust to what had happened. Wider relationships were affected and we needed to make lifestyle choices to take into account our new knowledge and understanding.'

## Rose's story

Rose ran a support group for mothers suffering with postnatal depression for several years. She has extensive knowledge of postnatal depression and has extended her skills in the field of applied life coaching and neuro-linguistic programming.

'I believe that personality plays a large part in the lives of women affected by postnatal depression. If the new mother is a naturally anxious person, having to look after a newborn, who relies on her for every need, tends to heighten her anxieties. There is nothing like anxiety to send your imagination wild! Wild imagination tends to produce panic and if we stay in a constant state of anxiety and panic, it often leads to panic attacks and depression. Mothers who take things lightly are less likely to be affected than the responsible perfectionist who wants to do really well and be the perfect mother.

'Prior to the baby arriving, she may well have had a dream of how it will be after the birth. In her dream, she saw herself as one of those women you see in the magazines, looking like a "yummy mummy" with a beautiful designer child, who eats, sleeps and makes eyes at his mummy. However, the reality is that she is exhausted, she cannot fit into any of her clothes, the baby wakes at all hours of the night and wants to be constantly fed or else it cries! It's not at all the picture she had in her head when she decided to have a baby.

'Some equate motherhood to that of a loss, a bereavement which is ironic when they have gained a baby. First of all they've lost their "bump". When they had their bump, everyone asked how they were and they had a lot of attention. Now that their bump has disappeared, everyone asks how the baby is and forgets them. They have lost their freedom, they can no longer go out freely if they want to. They may have lost their employment and the financial benefits that go with the job. They are according to them, "just a mum". Somehow they lose their identity and not even their body is their own as it is now a source of food for their infant.

'For a proportion of mothers, a traumatic delivery can terrorise the mother so much that it could trigger postnatal depression. These women suffer a form of postnatal depression induced by post-traumatic stress.

'One of the emotions felt by partners of sufferers is shock that their beautiful partner who was so looking forward to becoming a mother reacts that way. Many are frustrated and confused, others are angry, some are bewildered and don't know what to do for the best. Often they are very stressed and cannot understand what is happening in their lives.

'If they take good care of themselves, they will be more willing to take good care of their partners without feeling resentful and without feeling sorry for themselves. They have to keep in mind that this is only temporary and that six months or a year from now things will be very different. The best thing they can do for the sufferer is to understand what postnatal depression is all about and what they can do to help. They need to be loving, patient and understanding and not take anything personally. They need to develop a "thick skin".

'Antidepressants are very effective for some sufferers; however, I believe they are much more effective if used in conjunction with coaching, counselling or group therapy.

'Don't isolate yourself, things will only get worse if you do. Get enough rest. Don't overload or overbook yourself. If you are feeling down, call a friend and preferably arrange to meet, don't stay alone chewing over negative thoughts. Above all, remember that "this too shall pass" as well as "the best is yet to come".'

# Summing Up

- By the time you have reached this page you will know some important truths about yourself.

- You aren't alone and you aren't the first person to suffer with postnatal depression. Sadly, you won't be the last either.

- You know some of the reasons why you have postnatal depression and you will probably know for certain if you are suffering with the illness.

- Getting help as soon as possible is vital. You know where to go now.

- Make a recovery plan and try out as many ideas as possible. Don't discount any treatment or therapy until you have done your research.

- Talk endlessly to as many people as possible. Never be ashamed of postnatal depression.

- Know that you will get better and that all this will end.

- Finally, read this book over and over until it becomes part of you. I wish you luck on your trip through the clouds to the sunshine on the other side.

# Help List

## Association for Postnatal Illness (APNI)

145 Dawes Road, Fulham, London, SW6 7EB
Tel: 020 7386 0868
www.apni.org
A well-established charitable organisation, they aim to support sufferers, increase knowledge about the condition and promote ongoing research into the causes of postnatal depression. APNI have a very helpful website with a variety of information leaflets.

## Birth Trauma Association (BTA)

PO Box 671, Ipswich, Suffolk, IP1 9AT
www.birthtraumaassociation.org.uk
BTA supports all women who have had a traumatic birth experience.

## Depression Alliance

20 Great Dover Street, London, SE1 4LX
Tel: 0845 123 23 20
information@depressionalliance.org
www.depressionalliance.org
A leading UK charity which aims to raise awareness of depression and improve public services and support for sufferers.

## Homestart

Tel: 0800 068 63 68
www.home-start.org.uk
Homestart is a national treasure! They provide trained volunteers who will visit homes on a regular basis to relieve and support the mothers of babies and young children.

## Meet a Mum Association (MAMA)

54 Lillington Road, Radstock, BA3 3NR
Tel: 0845 120 3746 (helpline, Monday to Friday, 7-10pm)
MAMA provides friendship and support networks for mothers with postnatal depression. Their website is very informative.

## MIND

PO Box 277, Manchester, M60 3XN
Tel: 0845 766 0163 (helpline)
info@mind.org.uk
www.mind.org.uk
MIND addresses all forms of mental illness and offers some invaluable helpline services.

## NaPro Technology

www.naprotechnology.com
Features a good page dedicated to postnatal depression and Dr Katharina Dalton.

## National Childbirth Trust (NCT)

Tel: 0300 330 0772 (pregnancy and birth line)
Tel: 0300 330 0771 (breastfeeding line)
Tel: 0300 330 0773 (postnatal line)
Tel: 0300 330 0770 (enquiries line)
Tel: 0300 330 0774 (shared experiences line)
www.nctpregnancyandbabycare.com
NCT help over a million mums and dads each year through pregnancy, birth and early days of parenthood. They offer antenatal and postnatal courses, local support and reliable information to help all parents.

## Natural Progesterone Advisory Network

www.natural-progesterone-advisory-network.com
A comprehensive insight into the issue of hormone replacement as a treatment for postnatal depression.

## Netmums

www.netmums.co.uk
A great parenting resource with forums. They directly address and support members suffering with postnatal depression.

## Parentline Plus

Tel: 0808 800 222 (helpline)
www.parentlineplus.org.uk
Parenting guidance and advice tailor-made for mothers and fathers.

## Perinatal Illness – UK

PO Box 49769, London, WC1H 9WH
deb@pni-uk.com
www.pni-uk.com
A charity which addresses antenatal and postnatal illnesses, puerperal psychosis and birth trauma.

## PND Support

Tel: 800 043 2031 (helpline, Monday to Friday, 9am-7pm)
help@pndsupport.co.uk
www.pndsupport.co.uk
A warm and personal resource run by two former sufferers of postnatal depression.

## Progesterone Link

www.progesteronelink.com
You can find some information about progesterone therapy on this website.

## Relate

Tel: 0300 100 1234
www.relate.org.uk
Relate are the country's largest provider of relationship support – find more about the services they offer and where they're located via the website.

## Samaritans

Chris, PO Box 9090, Stirling, FK8 2SA
Tel: 08457 90 90 90
jo@samaritans.org
www.samaritans.org
This charity is a confidential source of emotional support.

## SANEline

1st Floor Cityside House, 40 Adler Street London E1 1EE
Tel: 0845 767 8000 (helpline)
www.sane.org.uk
A far-reaching organisation which raises awareness, assists research and
provides help and information for people with mental health issues.

# Book List

**Anxiety – The Essential Guide**
By Dr Jennifer Ashcroft, Need2Know, Peterborough, 2011.

**Complementary Therapies – The Essential Guide**
By Antonia Chitty and Victoria Dawson, Need2Know, Peterborough, 2011.

**Depression – The Essential Guide**
By Glenys O'Connell, Need2Know, Peterborough, 2009.

**Depression After Childbirth: How To Recognize, Treat and Prevent Postnatal Depression**
By Katharina Dalton and Wendy Holton, Oxford University Press, Oxford, 2001.

**Eyes Without Sparkle: A Journey Through Postnatal Illness**
By Elaine A Hanzak, Radcliffe, Oxford, 2005.

**Surviving Postnatal Depression: At Home No One Hears You Scream**
By Cara Aiken, Jessica Kingsley, London, 2000.

**The Terrible Twos – A Parent's Guide**
By Shanta Everington, Need2Know, Peterborough, 2010.

**Working Mothers – The Essential Guide**
By Denise Tyler, Need2Know, Peterborough, 2008.